MW01479702

<title>**HTML Activities**</title>
<h1>**Webtop Publishing on the Superhighway**</h1>

<h5>**by**</h5>

<h3>**Karl Barksdale**</h3>
<h3>**Eugene Paulsen**</h3>
<h3>**Gary Ashton**</h3>
<h3>**Earl Jay Stephens**</h3>

For use with
Notepad for Windows®
SimpleText for Macintosh®
Any Word Processor

With special support for Microsoft's® Internet Assistant for Word

JOIN US ON THE INTERNET
WWW: http://www.thomson.com
EMAIL: findit@kiosk.thomson.com   A service of I(T)P®

South-Western Educational Publishing
an International Thomson Publishing company I(T)P®

Cincinnati • Albany, NY • Belmont, CA • Bonn • Boston • Detroit • Johannesburg • London • Madrid
Melbourne • Mexico City • New York • Paris • Singapore • Tokyo • Toronto • Washington

ISBN: 0-538-67458-X

3 4 5 6 7 8 9 10 PR 01 00 99 98

Printed in the United States of America

Team Leader: Steve Holland
Editor: Becky E. Peveler
Consulting Editor: Catherine Duce
Marketing Manager: John Wills
Art Coordinator: Mike Broussard
Production Services: Electro-Publishing
Internal Design: Ann Small
Cover Design: Liz Harasymczuk

I(T)P ®

International Thomson Publishing

South-Western Educational Publishing is a division of International Thomson Publishing, Inc. The ITP logo is a registered trademark used herein under license by South-Western Educational Publishing.

Acknowledgments:

Consulting Editor:

Catherine Duce

Copy Editor:

Linda Allen — Good Guy Productions

Artwork:

Bill Heder

Art Acknowledgments:

Bill Heder — Internal Art

Candesa Interactive — Screen Shots

Mark Web Investigations for the pictures of Mark

State of Utah Resource Web pages 1 & 8

Reviewers:

Michael Rutter

Mike Seibert

Mark Ciampa

JOIN US ON THE INTERNET

WWW: **http://www.thomson.com**
E-MAIL: **findit@kiosk.thomson.com**

South-Western Educational Publishing is a partner in *thomson.com*, an on-line portal for the products, services, and resources available from International Thomson Publishing (ITP). Through our site, users can search catalogs, examine subject-specific resource centers, and subscribe to electronic discussion lists.

South-Western Educational Publishing is also a reseller of commercial software products. See our printed catalog or view this page at:

http://www.swpco.com/swpco/comp_ed/com_sft.html

For information on our products, visit our World Wide Web site at:

http://www.swpco.com/swpco.html

To join the South-Western Computer Education discussion list, send an e-mail message to: **majordomo@list.thomson.com** Leave the subject field blank, and in the body of your message key: SUBSCRIBE SOUTH-WESTERN-COMPUTER-EDUCATION <your e-mail address>.

A service of I(T)P ®

Preface

HTML and the World Wide Web provide a canvas to demonstrate your knowledge, skills, and abilities. HTML is an effective multimedia environment where you can show your creativity, express yourself on nearly any topic, and display your thoughts and talents in a variety of ways.

HTML Activities: Webtop Publishing on the Superhighway helps you learn HTML by providing interdisciplinary, multimedia activities for you to complete.

HTML is the official language of the World Wide Web (WWW or the Web). This book uncovers the mysterious hidden HTML tags that make communication on the World Wide Web possible.

If you have surfed the Web, you have seen many wonderful, and not so wonderful, Web pages in hyperspace. If you haven't surfed the Web, you will soon see how fantastic hyperspace (another name for the Web) can be. This book shows you how to design creative Web pages like the experts. It also explores the technology that makes the WWW possible.

Book Organization

HTML Activities is divided into three skill-building sections called Sectors:

Sector 1: HTML Quick Start gets you onto the Web fast! By completing the ten basic activities in this Sector, you learn the fundamentals of HTML.

Sector 2: The Tools of HTML Professionals builds your skill and confidence with HTML. This Sector introduces you to software tools called HTML Editors that make your HTML documents easier to create.

Sector 3: Webtop Publishing on the Superhighway investigates the artistry and technology behind the wonderful Web. This Sector explores advanced HTML features and examines the careers of professional Webmasters and Webtop publishers.

Each sector is divided into chapters and activities. The chapters provide background material for the hands-on activities included in the text.

This tutorial follows a very simple, step-by-step activity approach to learning HTML. Projects are short and to the point. You learn to use HTML by completing the activities that appear at the end of each chapter.

As you follow the activity steps, you will master the art of Webtop publishing.

And, as you will soon see, I — Mark Web, super-cyber investigative reporter for the Webtop Times — will be there to help you every step of the way!

Learn the Basics First

Like any other document, your Web pages will need troubleshooting, proofreading, editing, and improvement. Problems will arise that may require you to dissect your Web pages tag by tag. To do so, you MUST understand how HTML tags operate.

In the first Sector, you learn to create HTML tags with simple software tools that already exist on almost all computers.

The easiest way to learn how HTML tags work is to create a few Web pages with a simple text editor like **Notepad** in Windows or **SimpleText** on your Macintosh. In reality, most Web pages have either been created or edited in some way with these remarkably simple "word processoretts."

After you have a grasp of the basics, you can graduate to more sophisticated HTML Editors and Website building tools, such as:

Internet Assistant for Word
Netscape Gold
PageMill
Corel WordPerfect's Internet Publisher
HotMetal PRO
FrontPage

In addition to those listed above, there are many excellent HTML Editors that can make the job of creating wonderful Web pages much easier. Three different groups of HTML Editors are uncovered in Chapter 4. After that point, feel free to use the HTML tool of your choice. (You can continue to use Notepad or SimpleText as long as you like, but at some point, you may want to move to a professional HTML editing tool.)

What You Need to Use This Book

In Sector 1 you learn the basics of the HTML <TAG> system. It is essential to understand how <TAGS> work if you are to be a successful Web page developer. However, to be an accomplished Webtop Publisher, you must also learn to use a WYSIWYG HTML Editor. WYSIWYG is computer-speak for What You See Is What You Get. Internet Assistant for Word is a powerful WYSIWYG/HTML tool. Starting in Sector 2, you will learn to use this great piece of software.

Required:

To begin this tutorial, you need two user-friendly pieces of software. Most likely, they can already can be found on your computer:

- A text editor like **Notepad** (found in the Windows Accessories Group) or **SimpleText** (on any Macintosh). Any word processor will also work.
- A Web browser like Microsoft's **Internet Explorer** or the **Netscape Navigator**.

Optional:

There are a few optional items that will speed you along the Webtop superhighway:

- A connection to the World Wide Web and the Internet.
- Microsoft **Word**.
- Microsoft's **Internet Assistant for Word**.

If you have MS Word, you can download a copy of Internet Assistant free (See Chapter 4) at:

http://www.microsoft.com/msword/

If you don't have Word or an Internet connection, don't be alarmed! *You will be able to complete **all** the activities with Notepad or SimpleText.*

Using Microsoft's Internet Assistant for Word

Sector 2 provides a tutorial on how to use Microsoft's *Internet Assistant for Word* to enhance your Web pages (See Figure 0-1). The Internet Assistant is available free to Word users for the Windows and Macintosh platforms.

Microsoft's *Internet Assistant for Word* has some real advantages:

- First of all, it is a WYSIWYG HTML Editor.
- Second, Microsoft's Internet Assistant for Word turns your copy of Word for Windows

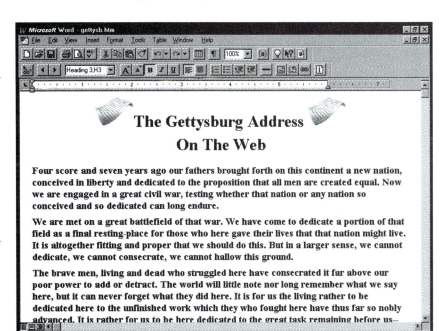

into an Internet browser! You can surf the Web and test your Web page creations from the same program. (However, if you wish, you can still use Microsoft's Internet Explorer or Netscape as your browser.)

- Third, you will be able to easily convert your existing Word documents into Web pages for publication on the World Wide Web.

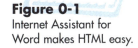

Figure 0-1
Internet Assistant for Word makes HTML easy.

The Internet Assistant can really help streamline the development of your Web pages. However, there are some real disadvantages (discussed in Chapter 1) to a beginner trying to learn HTML with a tool as powerful as the Internet Assistant for Word.

To offset these disadvantages, we recommend that you complete the first Sector of the book with a simple text editor like Notepad or SimpleText. Starting with the simpler tools will allow your HTML knowledge to increase at a faster pace.

Reading the Screen Shots: As Easy As A-B-C

For your convenience, most illustrations in this tutorial are actual screen shots, similar to Figure 0-2. These screen shots help you visualize the steps required to complete the activities. The steps are sequenced in alphabetical order. So, follow the letters. It is as easy as learning the A-B-C's, for example:

Step 1:   Hypertext links have three parts. To create a hypertext link:

1A: Key *The Disney Web Page*.

1B: Enter *http://www.disney.com/*.

1C: Click **OK**.

Figure 0-2
Creating a Hypertext Link:
A - Enter The Disney Web Page
B - Type http://www.disney.com/
C - Click OK

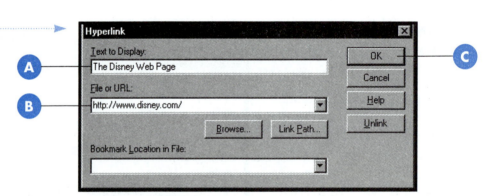

FAQs, Notes, and Hints

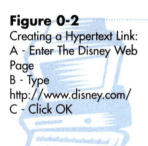

Don't let all of the terms, tags, and abbreviations of HTML and the World Wide Web scare you. We will teach you the terms and commands you need to know as we go along.

To assist you, we have included three helps:

* FAQs
* Notes
* Hints!

FAQs is an Internet acronym for Frequently Asked Questions. In this case, we mean Frequently Asked HTML Questions. **Notes** provide you with additional information you may wish to know. **Hints!** give you alternatives and short-cut options to the A-B-C, step-by-step instructions presented in the activities.

To help you with those troublesome high-tech words, there is a **Glossary** of terms available at the back of this book and on the *HTML Activities Web Page* at:

http://www.thomson.com/swpco/internet/markweb.html

Web Page Support

To further help you conquer HTML, there is an *HTML Activities Web Page* waiting for you on the Web. This Web page helps you access the resources used in this book. The Web page also directs you to some of the great Web pages in cyberspace. The *HTML Activities Web Page* (Figure 0-3) will keep you updated as HTML and the World Wide Web changes and improves. You will be able to find a bundle of things to help you with your activities:

- Graphics
- Multimedia support
- Software updates
- HTML news
- Glossary of terms

In Activity 4, we will show you how to find the *HTML Activities Web Page* at:

http://www.thomson.com/swpco/internet/markweb.html

Debriefings and Extensions

Debriefings appear at the end of each chapter. The Debriefings provide a time to reflect on what you have learned and to draw some conclusions from the master of HTML, Mark Web. Mark keeps notes full of helpful information.

Did you finish fast? Want some extra practice? Try the Extensions. In many of the activities, **Extensions** give you something new to try or something else to practice that extends beyond the regular activity. Give Extensions a try.

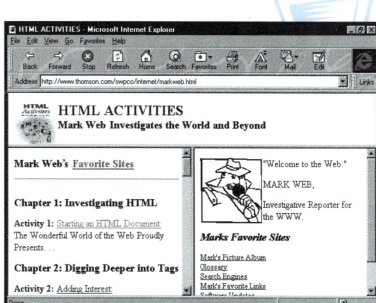

Figure 0-3
The *HTML Activities Web Page*

Tag Tables

As you will learn in Chapter 1, HTML is made up of tags. To help you remember the tags, a Table of Tags appears at the start of each activity. Also, a chapter-by-chapter **Tag Summary** can be found in Appendix A. If you forget a tag, you can look it up quickly in the Table of Tags by chapter, or you can go to the Tag Summary in Appendix A and review the tags there.

Table of Tags for Activity 1		
HTML Tags	<HTML></HTML>	Announces to the World Wide Web that this is an HTML document.
Header Tags	<HEAD></HEAD>	Lets you enter special information about your Web page.
Title Tags	<TITLE> </TITLE>	Places a short title or description in a browser's title bar.
Body Tags	<BODY></BODY>	Encloses the part of your Web page document that will actually be displayed by a Web browser. Anything not placed between the <BODY> tags will not be displayed properly.

Contents

**Sector
1**

Introduction

The Webtop Publishing Revolution

Mark Web Reporting

Zeeprrreee... And now to Mark Web, Investigative Reporter for the *HTML Webtop Times*. Mark...

"The way we communicate and share information constantly changes."

"People once used drums and smoke signals to send messages across sparsely inhabited valleys. Later, they wrote on rock walls, then on papyrus. People invented paper, wrote letters, and sent them by foot, boat, or horseback. As history moved along, new forms of information sharing were invented. Some of these inventions changed history and our lives forever. One of the life-changing inventions was the printing press."

"Johann Gutenberg created a printing press with moveable metal type containing letters, numbers, and symbols, and in 1454, printed multiple copies of a letter. The invention of the printing press allowed millions of inexpensive paper copies to be made quickly and easily. Gutenburg's press was the photocopy machine of the 15th century. Today, printing presses allow millions of books, newspapers, and magazines to be mass produced every day."

"Paper printing created huge new industries. Newspapers have billions of subscribers in every country. Billions of books, magazines, advertisements, and printed materials are constantly being reproduced. Millions of new jobs were created in this printed, paper-based communications industry."

"People like me, Mark Web, Investigative Reporter, used paper communications for ages. Billions of trees have given up their leafy lives satisfying the insatiable need to feed millions of printing presses, fax machines, photocopy machines, and printers around the world."

Figure 0-4:
Newspaper Rock State Park in Utah still holds messages from the ancient American past. Now you can view these rock art messages on the Web.

"In fact, here's an old photo of me sacrificing a tree limb to a hungry printer in an ancient human printing ritual!"

"Eventually, information sharing went electronic. The telegraph sped messages across continents. The telephone made voice-to-voice communication instantaneous. Radio, television, fax machine, e-mail, and video conferencing are new ways used to communicate and share information. Each of these electronic information-sharing devices were important steps in improving communication. (And, speaking for forests and trees everywhere — electronic communication is a major improvement.) The electronic telecommunications industry has altered our lives and employs millions and millions of people in high-tech jobs."

Webtop Publishing: The Next Big Step

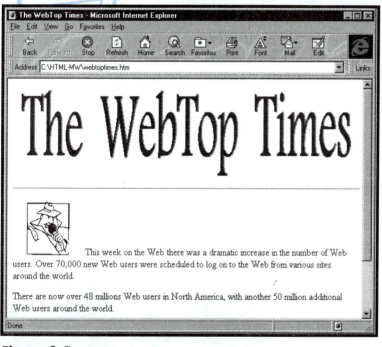

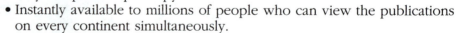

Figure 0-5:
"The WebTop Times" from the *HTML Activities Web Page*

The next very big, history-making, world-wide communications system has already been invented. It is called the World Wide Web. This phase of human communication also employs millions of people who use the Web to share data and information.

The Internet and the World Wide Web created a revolution in the way we share information. We are now publishing magazines, newspapers, and books electronically and distributing the information instantly to computers around the world on the Web. (See Figure 0-5.)

Electronic publishing on the Web has many advantages over paper publishing. Webtop publications are:

- Very inexpensive per copy.
- Instantly available to millions of people who can view the publications on every continent simultaneously.
- Changeable (they can be updated) at a moment's notice. (Try changing an article in a newspaper after it is printed!)
- Electronic, saving the lives of countless trees.

More importantly, Webtop publishing is fun to do. Webtop publishing is a new, fast-growing communications industry, creating millions of new jobs. The Web is a place where electronic publishers of all kinds, sizes, and styles can coexist and thrive.

With the help of this tutorial, you will become a Webtop publisher in a matter of weeks.

The Financial Side of Webtop Publishing

Webtop publishing is fun, and it can also be rewarding. New jobs are developing in every community that require Webtop publishing skills and abilities. Take a look at the Web today. Someone created every page. Many of the best corporate, government, and university pages were created by professionals who were paid for their creativity and skill.

While getting a good job is a good reason to learn Webtop publishing, it is an added benefit for those who already love the creativity of this new interactive industry.

The Creative Side of Webtop Publishing

You can become your own electronic publisher. You can create publications that go beyond simple words by including a variety of multi-media effects to communicate your messages, such as:

- Graphics
- Video
- Sound
- Animation

Webtop publishing can be done by anybody with a minimum of practice. *In fact, you already know a lot about Webtop publishing.* That's right. You can incorporate many things you already know and apply them to your Webtop publications. Some examples are:

- Writing skills
- Artistic skills
- Word processing skills
- Desktop publishing skills
- Computer skills
- Knowledge gained from course work in science, math, social science, business education, language arts or any other subject
- Personal experience
- Information about your hobbies and interests

In later reports, Mark Web will explain more about HTML — the language of the Web and the key to Webtop publishing. You will also learn about the World Wide Web, Web browsers, and some very important Webtop publishing tools called HTML Editors.

With so many fun things to do, what are you waiting for? Turn to Chapter 1 and start saving forests by creating publications for the wonderful world of the Web.

HTML Quick Start

HTML is the language of the World Wide Web. HTML allows you to create Web pages stored on hundreds of thousands of computers all over the planet.

Web pages, like those you will soon create, started a new electronic publishing phenomenon. The number of people reading Web pages grows by tens of thousands every week.

Just as the personal computer became an integral part of our lives in the 1980's, the World Wide Web (the Web) became an essential tool linking people together in the 1990's. With just your PC, your digital world was limited to your computer's desktop. With the Web, your digital boundaries stretch around the globe, limited only by the speed of your modem.

Also known by the letters WWW, the Web touches major parts of our lives. The WWW is a crucial component in the communications strategies for thousands of businesses, schools, and governmental agencies. For example, every government agency is on the Web. Nearly every school is connected to the Web (or is making plans to do so.) Businesses use the Web to communicate with customers, train employees, and inform shareholders. New Web-related jobs have been created in many industries, including computing, telecommunications, advertising, publishing, retail, and core manufacturing industries. Even food stores and fast food restaurants take orders over the Web.

For many people, learning to use HTML is an essential communications skill.

In Chapter **1** *Investigating HTML* gives you a quick start using HTML to create Web pages.

In Chapter **2** *Digging Deeper into HTML Tags* goes to the heart of HTML formatting tags. Formatting tags are the building blocks of HTML Web pages.

In Chapter **3** *Searching for Clues* takes you to the World Wide Web to investigate some great Web pages. In Chapter 3, you create hypertext links and begin transforming simple Web pages into Webtop publications.

Sector 1

Investigating HTML

This chapter gets you started creating Web pages, and in the process of creating, you will learn to use HTML.

HTML is a document description language — it describes how a document should be displayed by a Web browser. HTML uses "tags" to "mark up" documents. These tags allow an interpreter, like a Web browser, to display document information, like text and graphics, in the form of Web pages.

Don't worry about any special tools in this first section. Your computer already has a simple text editor you can use. You can start with Notepad, SimpleText, or any word processor. Later, you may wish to upgrade to more powerful HTML development tools called HTML Editors. But for now, keep it simple. Keeping it simple makes it easier for you to learn the concepts behind the creation of great Web pages.

Here are a few questions that will be answered in this chapter:

- What are HTML tags?
- How do HTML tags work?
- What is a text editor?
- What is an HTML Editor?
- Why do I need a Web browser?

Creating Web pages isn't hard, as you will soon see.

O b j e c t i v e s :

- Discover the meaning of HTML.
- Define the World Wide Web.
- See how tags work.
- Learn what browsers do.
- Review the four HTML starting tags.
- Create an HTML folder on your hard drive or on floppy disk.
- Investigate how to save text files with the .htm or .html extension.

FAQs

What is the World Wide Web?

The World Wide Web (WWW or "the Web" for short) is a collection of computers all over the world that speak HTML. These computers contain Web pages and make them available to Web users. Web host computers are called **servers.** A new Web server connects to the Web every ten minutes. There are millions and millions of Web documents on these tens of thousands of Web servers. There is no single center of the Web. In fact, it can be said that wherever you are is the center of a growing World Wide Web of information.

What HTML Really Means (the shocking details)

"Hi! My name is Mark Web."

"I am reporting to you today on the hidden topic…the hidden <tags> of HTML."

"**HTML** is an acronym, or a word made up of letters from several words. In this case, HTML is an acronym for **HyperText Markup Language**. Let's break these three words down to discover their meaning."

"Let's start with **Language**. HTML is the language of the Web, just like German is the language of Germany and Croatian is the language of Croatia. HTML is what Web browsers (like Netscape or the Internet Explorer) use to interpret and display documents on the World Wide Web."

"**Hypertext** is a term applied to words that take you somewhere. For example, if you were to click your mouse on this "Rock Art" icon (or picture) located on my Web page in a big city like Cincinnati, Ohio, (see Figure 1-1)…Zing!"

"…you would be taken on a hypertext jump through cyberspace (the Internet) to a Web page of Native American Rock Art near the remote and isolated Newspaper Rock State Park, Utah. (See Figure 1-2.) When you use hypertext, you can go almost anywhere at the speed of electricity. It's positively electric!"

Figure 1-1

Rock Art icon *courtesy of the SURWEB project*

"The last word, **Markup**, is the key term. If you were to take a big, fat, felt-tip pen and draw all over the pages of this book, you would be accused of "marking up the book." (The Native Americans who carved Newspaper Rock were accused of marking up rock walls.) Well, that is exactly what markup means. Web pages are marked up by little tags in angle brackets < >. These tags tell Web browsers, like the Internet Explorer (Figure 1-2) or the Netscape Navigator (Figure 1-3), how to display Web pages so you and I can read them."

Messages from the past

Figure 1-2
Newspaper Rock State Park in Utah

"Here is an example. This is my Web page. It looks like the picture in Figure 1-3."

"However, if you look underneath the page at the hidden HTML tags, the page looks like Figure 1-4."

"See the tags? Shocking, isn't it! These tags literally mark up the text. The tags create a language spoken by Web browsers and Web servers. The tags tell the browsers how to display Web pages.

"And Web pages will display on any type of computer! Take a close look at Figures 1-2 and 0-4. As you can see, the same pictures and Web pages can display on both Macintosh and Windows computers! You will see both Windows and Macintosh pictures in this book, because on the Web, it doesn't matter what kind of computer you are using. This is a very cool thing about HTML. No matter what kind of computer you have, if you have a Web browser, you can read HTML Web pages."

"Without HTML tags, a Web page would look very sad indeed. Also, if the tags are not entered correctly, a page will display defectively (See Figure 1-5). Sometimes defective Web pages won't display at all!"

Note: The truth about tags: HTML tags are rambunctious. Always ready to work, tags consider Web browsers to be lazy. Tags actually feel that they do all the work and Web browsers get all the credit. Quite understandably, Web browsers take offense...

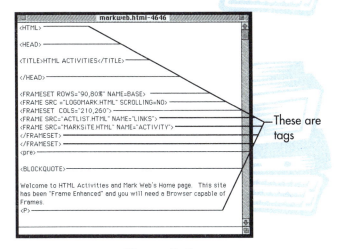

Figure 1-3
The Official Mark Web Page

Figure 1-4
The Hidden HTML Tags

Tag . . . you're on display!

HTML tags make Webtop publishing possible. HTML uses a bunch of tags to display information in different ways. There are a few quick things you should remember about tags:

- There are two kinds of tags; **open** and **close**.
- **Open** tags are easy to spot. Just look for the angle (< >) brackets.
- **Close** tags have a slash after the first bracket (</ >).
- **Tags** normally appear in pairs.

Figure 1-5
This Web Page Contains Tag Errors

FAQs

What is a Web Browser?

A Web browser is a software tool that searches and displays HTML pages on the WWW. Think of a Web browser as a translator that converts HTML into a language you and I can understand. There are lots of Web browsers around. The most widely used browsers are the Netscape Navigator and Microsoft's Internet Explorer. Each of these has both Macintosh and Windows versions.

We have used a variety of browsers in this book to demonstrate that HTML and the Web work with any kind of browser and on different types of computers. There are minor differences in how things are displayed. Review the following browsers:

- Internet Explorer for Windows
  (See Figure 1-2)

- Internet Explorer for Macintosh
  (See Figure 1-5)

- Netscape Navigator for Windows
  (See Figure 1-3)

- Netscape Navigator for Macintosh
  (See Figure 0-4)

With that background, a single example can show you how tags work. The <CENTER> tag displays any text between the tags in the center of the page, like this:

<CENTER>Mark Web</CENTER>

The open <CENTER> tag starts centering the words and the close </CENTER> tag stops centering the text. That's all there is to it! HTML is very easy to understand.

There are many other tags. Some tags make words bigger <H1> or smaller <H6>. Other tags can make words blink <BLINK>. Some tags create lists <UL><LI></LI></UL>. Some tags even search for new Web pages <A HREF=" "></A>. There are a zillion tags you can use in your Webtop documents.

One last reminder, HTML tags usually consist of two tags; a *beginning* or *open* tag, and an ending or *close* tag. The close tag is easily identified by a slash </> as in </CENTER>.

Starting Tags

Every HTML document starts out with the same basic HTML tags called *starting tags*. These starting tags frame an HTML document much like a frame surrounds a picture or a fence surrounds a yard. Every Web page needs to contain the starting tags.

A basic set of starting tags includes the tags shown below in the following order:

```
<HTML>
<HEAD><TITLE> </TITLE></HEAD>
<BODY>
</BODY>
</HTML>
```

These four tags give structure and organization to Web pages.

The first or *open* tag <HTML> wakes up your Web browser and tells it to start translating the HTML tags and displaying the Web page. The last tag </HTML> is the *close* tag. This tag tells your browser, "Go to sleep. The Web page is being displayed. Your work is done."

The <HEAD> is the heading of the Web page. This is a good place for notes and information about the Web page because whatever you put in this section is usually <u>NOT</u> displayed. (See Figure 1-6.) You can end the heading with the close heading tag </HEAD>.

The <TITLE> tag puts the title of the Web page in the title bar at the top of the Web browser as shown in Figure 1-7. The <TITLE> tags are placed between the <HEAD> tags.

The <BODY></BODY> tags markup the information that <u>IS</u> displayed in the main browser window. If it isn't in between the body, it can't be seen by Web page readers.

Starting tags organize a Web page for a Web browser. For example, here is how one of Aesop's Fables appears in HTML.[1]

Look for the starting tags!

HTML open tag ——
Head Tags ——
Title between tags ——

Body Tags

HTML close Tag

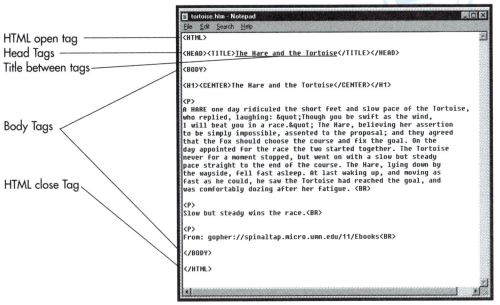

Figure 1-6
Aesop's Fable, "The Hare and the Tortoise" with HTML Tags

Here is how the story of the Hare and the Tortoise will look on the Web in a Web browser. (Figure 1-7.)

Title Bar ——

Title ——

Body ——

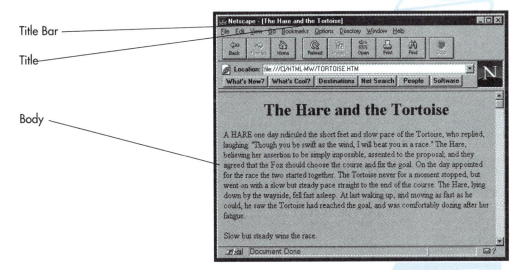

Figure 1-7
"The Hare and the Tortoise" Display in a Browser

Uppercase or Lowercase? That is the Question

Tags can be either uppercase <CENTER> or lowercase <center>. It doesn't matter which case you use. Some Webtop publishers like tags in capital letters <TITLE> so they can spot the tags easily. Others prefer small letters <title> so they can read the words effortlessly. The case you use is up to you.

---

[1] The Gutenberg project: gopher://spinaltap.micro.umn.edu/11/Ebooks/By%20Title/aesop

The Story of the Text Editor and the Browser

Before you begin Activity 1, review five essential details:

1. Starting **application programs** on your computer.

2. Creating a **folder** in which to save your HTML Webtop publications. (You can create this folder on your hard drive or on a floppy disk.)

3. Finding a simple **Text Editor**.

4. **Saving** your Web documents **As** simple **ASCII (DOS) Text** with the **.htm** or **.html** extension.

5. Finding your **Web browser** and opening your HTML file.

Let's take care of these basics one at a time.

1. Starting Application Programs in Your Version of Windows or on Your Macintosh

Most programs require a click or a double-click to start. If you don't know how to start application programs on your computer, review your Windows or Macintosh documentation. Better yet, get someone to show you.

2. Creating a Folder (Or a Directory) Where You Can Save Your HTML Web Pages

Clean off an old dusty floppy disk, format it, and save your Web pages on it. Or, if possible, create a folder on your hard drive or network drive called HTML-??. The ?? is for your initials. Your initials are important if other people use the same computer you do. For example, I, Mark Web, Investigative Reporter have named my folder:

HTML-MW

Your folder/directory or floppy will help keep your Webtop creations safe. Folders are called directories or subdirectories in older versions of Windows, in UNIX, or on old DOS machines. Since the release of Windows 95, the word "folders" has become acceptable to use. Macintosh users have always used the term "folders." Think of it this way — save your Webtop publications in a file folder named HTML-?? on your computer (see Figure 1-8).

Create a folder or directory of your own

Figure 1-8
Mark Web's official HTML-MW folder.

3. Finding a Simple Text Editor

Web pages are created with text editors. Text editors are to Web pages what bees are to making honey. (Without them, you don't get anything.)

A text editor is a simple word processor that saves your words in a text format that browsers can read. There are millions of busy text editors cranking out lots of Web pages that Web surfers browse.

Notepad for Windows is an excellent simple text editor (see Figure 1-9a). On a Macintosh, **SimpleText** will do the trick (see Figure 1-9b). You will want to graduate to more sophisticated HTML editors later (see Chapter 3), but not to start with.

Figure 1-9a
Notepad Icon in Windows

Starting your HTML experience with SimpleText or Notepad will give you the ability to think like a pilot, not a passenger. You will be able to:

- Identify problems on Web pages
- Fix problems without causing more problems
- Work with confidence on unfamiliar computers (which often happens in the Webtop publishing business)
- Read the hidden HTML tags from interesting pages all over the world
- Analyze new techniques, tags, and HTML tricks from Web pages found on the WWW
- Fly solo, without an HTML flight instructor, like me, Mark Web, to help you along.

Figure 1-9b
SimpleText Icon on a Mac

For these reasons, Activities 1 through 10 are to be done with SimpleText, Notepad, or some other simple text editor. Once you feel comfortable at the HTML controls, you can easily complete Activities 11 through 23 with the help of a powerful HTML Editor.

4. **Saving a Simple ASCII Text with an .htm or .html Extension**

    Notepad and SimpleText automatically save your Web pages as simple ASCII text. Simply select **Save As** from the **File** menu and name your file.

    When naming HTML files, remember that your browser looks for files that end in .html or .htm. These are called **extensions**. You must use the extension **.htm** when saving HTML Web pages in DOS and in early versions of Windows. (Figure 1-10a.) The longer **.html** extension can be used by Macintosh, with Windows 95 or higher, and on UNIX computers. (Figures 1-10b, 1-10c).

    Your word processor can also be a text editor. If you use Word or WordPerfect, save your Web page as a simple ASCII Text document by choosing the text format options in your Save As dialog box. There are several ways to do this, but remember, in each of the examples that follow the file will be an ASCII Text file with a .htm or .html extension:

    - In Figure 1-10a, the document is being saved in Word for Windows 95 as a **.htm** file in an HTML format.
    - In Figure 1-10b, the file is being saved as a **Text Export** in WordPerfect on a Macintosh computer with a **.html** extension.
    - Finally, in Figure 1-10c, the file is being saved as a **.html** file in Windows for WordPerfect as a text file.

FAQs

What is ASCII?

SCII is an acronym for <u>A</u>merican <u>S</u>tandard <u>C</u>ode for <u>I</u>nformation <u>I</u>nterchange. It simply means that all you get is plain and simple text like the letters on your keyboard. All of the special formatting commands inside the document are eliminated. Only the simple keyboard-like letters remain. HTML tags are made up of text or ASCII characters.

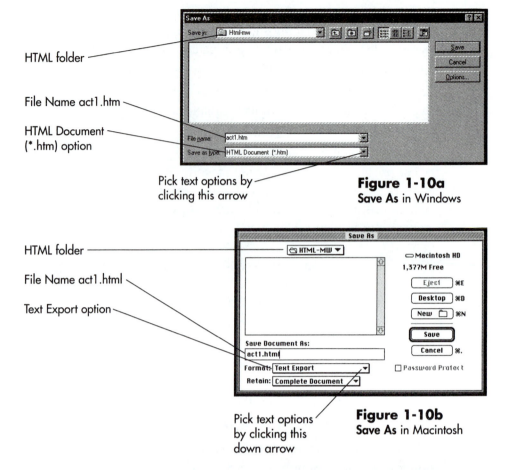

HTML folder

File Name act1.htm

HTML Document (*.htm) option

Pick text options by clicking this arrow

Figure 1-10a
Save As in Windows

HTML folder

File Name act1.html

Text Export option

Pick text options by clicking this down arrow

Figure 1-10b
Save As in Macintosh

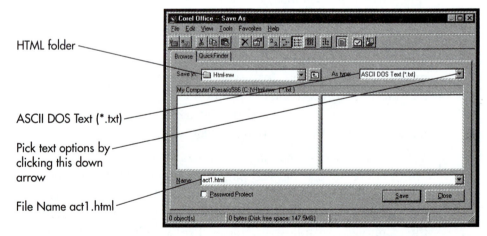

HTML folder

ASCII DOS Text (*.txt)

Pick text options by clicking this down arrow

File Name act1.html

Figure 1-10c
Save As in WordPerfect for Windows

5. **Finding Your Web Browser and Opening Your .htm or .html File**

You will need to start your Web browser before you can view your HTML creations. Chances are, you already have a Web browser somewhere on your computer's hard drive or on your local area network that you can use. If not, you can download a browser from either Netscape Communications Corporation, the

National Center for Supercomputing Applications, or Microsoft Corporation. Visit the *HTML Activities Web Page* (Activity 4) to learn the location of these various download sites.

Your Web browser is used to test and preview your Web page creations. If you have Windows 95 or higher, or a newer version of Windows NT, you already have a copy of Microsoft's browser, the Internet Explorer, somewhere on your computer or network. If you are using the Internet Assistant for Word, Word itself can become your browser. (See Sector 2.)

Internet service providers like America Online, Prodigy, AT&T Worldnet, or CompuServe can supply you with a Web browser.

When you find your browser, jot down the folder or directory that holds your browser application file so you can find and open it. In Activity 1, you will learn how to open your HTML Web page files in your browser.

Debriefing

To review, HTML is short for Hypertext Markup Language. HTML is the official language of the World Wide Web. HTML uses codes called tags that tell a Web browser (like Netscape or Microsoft Internet Explorer) how to display a document for Web surfers to see. The tags display information in a way you can read it. For example, the <CENTER> tag will center information on the browser window, and the <TITLE> tag will put the title of your Web page in the title bar of a Web browser.

To view your Web page creations, you need a Web browser. You also need a text editor to enter your HTML tags. Text editors save HTML Web pages as simple ASCII text. You need to add the following extension to your file names:

- For Windows 3.1 and earlier, use a **.htm** file extension
- For Macintosh and Windows 95 or higher, use a **.html** file extension

It is a good idea to create a folder or directory where you can save your HTML Webtop creations safely. Name your folder HTML-??. The ?? is where you can place your initials. Your initials are only important if you share a computer. If you can't save on your computer's hard drive or network drive, format a floppy disk and save your HTML documents there. Be careful to save properly. It would be a shame to have all your Webtop creations disappear by accident.

One last thing — don't forget to make backup copies of important Webtop publications.

he Wonderful World of the Web Proudly Presents . . .

The easiest way to learn HTML is to try it. All you need to start is an Internet browser like Netscape's Navigator, or Microsoft's Internet Explorer, and a very simple text editor like Notepad for Windows or SimpleText for the Macintosh. If you wish, you may even use your word processor as your text editor.

In this activity, you are going to introduce yourself to the Web by creating a simple Web page in a text editor and displaying it in a Web browser. You don't need to be hooked up to the Internet or World Wide Web to do this. In fact, nothing could be simpler.

Before you begin, review the Table of Tags for Activity 1. These tags must appear in every Web page and are often called the "starting tags."

Notice that each of the "starting tags" consists of a pair of tags. The first tag <TITLE> is called the opening or **open** tag. The second tag </TITLE> is called the closing or **close** tag. Both the opening and closing tags are enclosed by angle brackets < >.

Inside the angle brackets is a command word. For example, the *open* tag starts the <BODY> command, and the *close* tag ends the body command by adding a slash </BODY>.

Table of Tags for Activity 1		
HTML Tags	<HTML></HTML>	Announces to the World Wide Web that this is an HTML document.
Header Tags	<HEAD></HEAD>	Lets you enter special information about your Web page.
Title Tags	<TITLE> </TITLE>	Places a short title or description in a browser's title bar.
Body Tags	<BODY></BODY>	Encloses the part of your Web page document that will actually be displayed by a Web browser. Anything not placed between the <BODY> tags will not be displayed properly.

O b j e c t i v e s

- Start Notepad, SimpleText, or your word processor.
- Enter the starting HTML tags listed in the Table of Tags for Activity 1.
- Save your first HTML Web page.
- Test or view your Web page in a browser like Netscape or Internet Explorer.

Activity 1 Starting an HTML Document

Step 1: Start Windows Notepad or Macintosh SimpleText. All it usually takes is a click or a double-click on the icons shown in Figures A1-1a or A1-1b.

Figure A1-1a:
The Windows Notepad
Icon

Figure A1-1b:
The Macintosh SimpleText
Icon

Note: You may use a word processor or an HTML Editor of your choice to complete these activities.

Step 2: A blank page should appear. If you don't have a blank page, select **File**, **New**.

Step 3: Start your Web page by entering your starting tags as shown below and in Figure A1-2.
Hint! Press your Caps Lock key to enter capital letters.

    <HTML>
    <HEAD><TITLE> </TITLE></HEAD>
    <BODY>
    </BODY>
    </HTML>

Figure A1-2:
Enter the Starting Tags

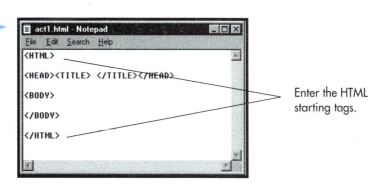

Enter the HTML
starting tags.

Step 4: To add text in your new HTML Web page:

4A: Click your mouse between the <TITLE></TITLE> tags and type your first name followed by **Web Page** as in **Mark's Web Page** (as shown in Figure A1-3).

4B: Click your mouse between the body tags and enter the following text as shown in Figure A1-3. Fill in the blanks with your personal information about where you were born and where you live:

Hi! My name is _____.

I live in (Insert the name of the city and state/province or country in which you live).

I was born in (Insert the name of the city and state/province or country in which you were born).

I (Say something about yourself.)

Figure A1-3:
Mark's Web Page Text
and Tags
A - Enter your title
B - Enter in your personal
information

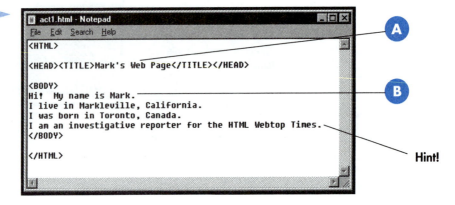

Figure A1-3:
Mark's Web Page Text
and Tags
A - Enter your title
B - Enter in your personal
information

FAQs

What personal information should NOT be shared on the Web?

ou shouldn't share any specifics about yourself, like your phone number or street address. Keep your personal information fairly general and include only your first name, state, province, region, and city.

Hint!   Word processors wrap text to the next line when you reach the end of a line. Some text editors may not have a wraparound feature like on your word processor. You can type your HTML Web page on a single line if you like. However, it will be very hard to read, correct, and edit. With HTML Text Editors, press Enter or Return at the end of each line. (You don't have to do this in a typical word processor.) In Notepad, you can turn on the wraparound feature by selecting WordWrap from the Edit menu.

Note: Remember, since the characters created when you press Return/Enter are not ASCII characters, HTML will take no notice of where you press Return/Enter and will organize your text the way it looks best in a Web browser, as shown in Figures A1-9a and b on page 20.

Step 5:   To save your new HTML Web page:

5A: Click **Save As** from the **File** pull-down menu as shown in Figure A1-4.

Figure A1-4:
The File Menu
A - Click Save As.

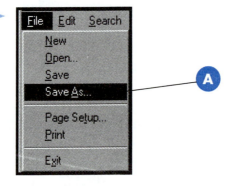

5B: Select the drive and folder (or directory) where you are going to save your HTML document. (In Figure A1-5a, the Web document will be saved in the C:\html-?? folder on a Windows 95 computer. In Figure A1-5b, the file will be saved in the HTML-?? folder on a Macintosh computer.)

Hint! Remember the ?? in HTML-?? is for your initials. For example, Mark Web's folder is HTML-MW.

5C: Enter a file name for your document. Key **act1.html** on Macintosh or in Windows 95, or key **act1.htm** in Windows 3.1.

Note: All of your documents should end with **.htm** in DOS and Windows or **.html** on a Macintosh. (Windows 95 or higher systems will accept both **.htm** and **.html**.)

5D: Make sure you save the document as TEXT. Text files can be called several things including: Text Document, ASCII DOS Text, or ANSI DOS TEXT. (Review Chapter 1 and Figures 1-10a, 1-10b, and 1-10c if you need help.)

5E: Click **Save** or **OK** when you are finished.

Figure A1-5a:
Save As in Windows
B - Select your HTML-?? folder
C - Enter act1.htm
D - Select Text or HTML document
E - Click Save]

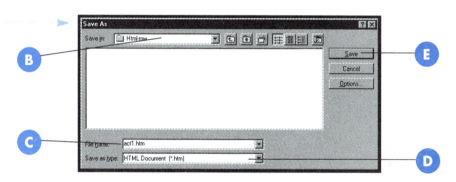

Figure A1-5b:
Save As on a Macintosh
B - Select your HTML-?? folder
C - Enter act1.html
E - Click Save

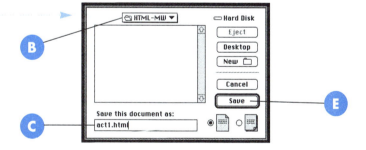

FAQs

What are truncated file names?

DOS and early Windows programs limited file names to 8 characters with a 3 character extension (8.3 characters). For example, **business.doc** (8.3) is a good file name. But, **important.document** was too long (9.8 characters) and therefore not a legal file name. This file name would be shortened (or truncated) to **importan.doc** or even **import~1.doc.** The file **act1.html** may be shortened to **act1.htm**. Macintosh computers never had this limitation.

Step 6: To view and test your **act1.html** or **act1.htm** document:

6A: Open your Web browser.

6B: Click on the **File** menu.

6C: In the Internet Explorer, select **Open** (Figure A1-6a), then skip to Step 6D.

In Netscape, select the **Open File** (Figure A1-6b), then skip to Step 6E.

Figure A1-6a
The Internet Explorer File Menu
A - Click Open

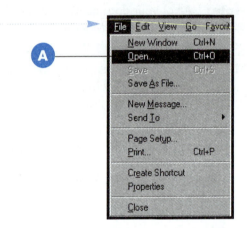

Figure A1-6b
The Netscape File Menu
A - Click Open File

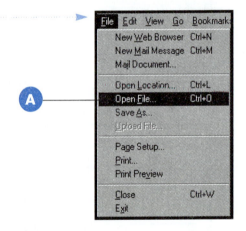

6D: With the Internet Explorer:

1. Click the **Browse** button as marked in Figure A1-7.

2. Find your HTML-?? folder as indicated in Figure A1-8a.

3. Select your file **act1.html** or **act 1.htm**.

4. Select Open.

5. Click OK.

Figure A1-7
Finding your HTML File
using Internet Explorer
1 - Click Browse
2 - Search for HTML-??
folder
3 - Select the act1.html or
act1.htm file
4 - Click Open
5 - Click OK

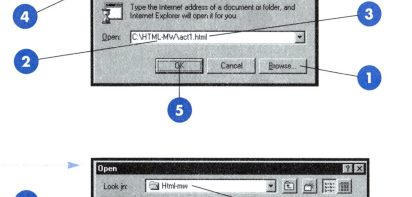

Figure A1-8a
The Internet Explorer
Open Window
1 - Search for HTML-??
folder
2 - Select the act1.html or
act1.htm file
3 - Click Open

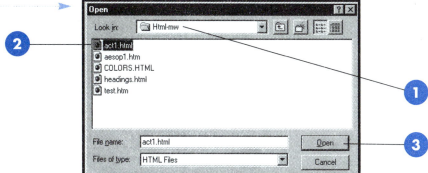

6E: In Netscape, find your **act1.html** or **act1.htm** file by opening the HTML-?? folder where you saved your Web page as in Figures A1-8a or A1-8b.

Figure A1-8b
The Netscape Open
Window in Macintosh
1 - Search for HTML-??
folder
2 - Select the act1.html or
act1.htm file
3 - Click Open

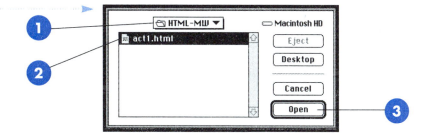

Step 7: View your Web page and look for errors. Your publication will appear as shown in Figure A1-9a or 9b. Review the HTML tags displayed in your document. Notice the following:

1. The <TITLE></TITLE> tags place your name in the browser's Title Bar.

2. The <BODY></BODY> tags place information in the main browser window where you can read it easily.

Figure A1-9a
Your First Web Page in
Internet Explorer
1 - The <TITLE>
2 - The <BODY>

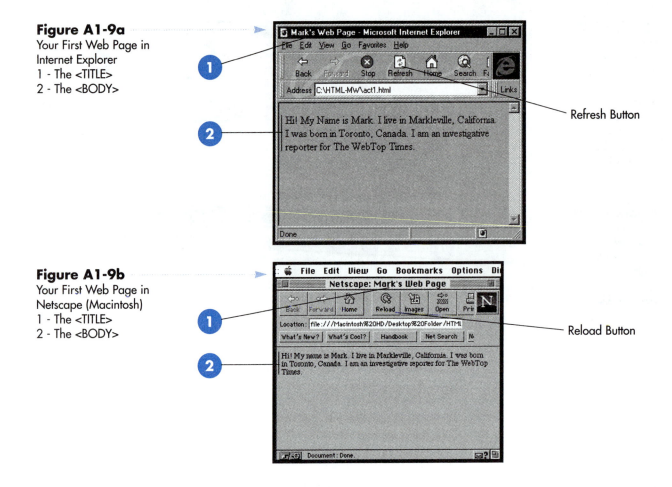

Refresh Button

Figure A1-9b
Your First Web Page in
Netscape (Macintosh)
1 - The <TITLE>
2 - The <BODY>

Reload Button

FAQs

Why display this activity with different browsers on different computers?

We have used two different browsers on two different kinds of computers to demonstrate an important point. First, HTML doesn't care which kind of computer you use or if you use Netscape or Internet Explorer or some other browser. It still displays your HTML Web page effectively. Second, different Web browsers do display the same information in slightly different ways. For example, notice that your browser sizes the text to fit the size of your browser window. You can change the size of your browser window and see how the text will display itself so you can still read every word. For example, the browser in Figure A1-9a is narrower, so the first line ends with *California*. In Figure A1-9b, the browser window is wider and the first line ends after the word *born*. As a Webtop publisher, you must be aware of how different browsers display information, since you may never know the kind of browser your Webtop reader may have.

Fixing Mistakes

If you make a mistake and the Web page doesn't look the way you intended, you can go back and fix your Web page in your text editor. There are a couple of things to remember:

- When you are finished making corrections, you must **save** your Web page as a text file before you retest it. Remember the **.htm** or **.html** extensions.
- If your text editor is looking for **.txt** or Text files, change the type to **.htm**, **.html**, or to **All** document types.
- Browsers usually save copies of recently opened Web pages in a special memory cache on your computer. If you change your HTML Web page, you may not be able to view the new changes unless you clear the cache or restart your browser. But, there may be a better way. Most browsers have a **Refresh** (Internet Explorer Figure A1-9a) or **Reload** (Netscape Figure A1-9b) button that reloads the original copy of the Web page. Try the Reload or Refresh button.
- Look for missing brackets or brackets facing the wrong way (>BODY<).
- Make sure your close tags have a slash (/).

Step 8:

Exit your Web browser and your text editor by clicking the close box on each open window or by clicking the **File** menu and clicking **Exit** in Windows or **Close** on the Macintosh.

Debriefing

Congrats! You have just created your first HTML Web page! In the activities that follow, you will be able to improve and enhance your pages and watch them improve from simple Web documents to full-fledged Webtop publications.

Here are my official HTML notes from this activity:

1. To start a new Web page, find and open your text editor.

2. Enter the starting tags as shown here:

   <HTML>

   <HEAD><TITLE> </TITLE></HEAD>

   <BODY>

   </BODY>

   </HTML>

3. Anything you key between the <TITLE></TITLE> tags appears in a browser's Title Bar.

4. Information you want the browser to display must be placed between the <BODY></BODY> tags.

5. If you make a change in your Web page, always **save** before you **retest** a Web page. Use the **Reload** (Netscape) or **Refresh** (Internet Explorer) button to see your updates.

6. Save your HTML Web pages as one of these:
   - Text Document
   - ASCII DOS TEXT
   - ANSI DOS TEXT
   - HTML (.htm)
   - HTML (.html)

7. Save with the **.html** extension for Window 95 or higher computers and for Macintosh computers. Save as **.htm** on Windows 3.1 computers..

Digging Deeper into HTML Tags

Formatting Tags Add Interest to Simple Web Pages!

In Activity 1 you learned to create a simple Web page by entering starting tags into a document. In this chapter, you will open the file you created (act1.html) and add new tags that make your simple Web pages much more interesting.

Tags that add interest are called **formatting tags**. Formatting tags can make any document appear organized. Formatting tags tell your Web browser how to display a page of information in an interesting way.

Most text documents have very similar parts. They usually have headings, paragraphs, words, and pages. Over hundreds of years of writing, humans have created certain styles for documents to enhance their appearance and to make them easy to read.

This chapter introduces you to some of the tags the Web uses to display text in ways that are familiar to the average reader.

O b j e c t i v e s :

- Discover what formatting tags do.
- Use the following formatting tags:
- Center tags
- Heading tags 1 to 6
- Paragraph and break tags
- Ordered list tags
- Unordered list tags

Format, Format, Who Knows the Format Tags?

"Okay. You deserve to be congratulated on a fine start. You have learned to use a text editor, enter starting tags, and create and view a Web page."

"But, let's be honest. It isn't beautiful (Figures A1-9a and A1-9b). It's hardly the stuff that Webtop publishing is made of. It's time to take the next step and learn about formatting tags."

"You are probably familiar with the term "formatting" from your word processing lessons. When you format a page, you can change the margins, bold a heading, create an indention, and add other effects to your word processing document. The purpose of formatting is to make your document easier to read."

"It is the same with HTML documents. Sprucing up your HTML document, act1.html, requires the expert use of a few simple formatting tags. Let's start with an easy one — the <CENTER> tag."

The <CENTER> Tag

The <CENTER> tag is one of the easiest formatting tags to understand. We center text all of the time on letters, reports, in books, and in magazines. The Web is no different. For example:

<CENTER>This tag places text in the</CENTER>
<CENTER>center of the Web page.</CENTER>

Remember to use the close tag </CENTER> to stop centering or else

. . . everything
on the page
will be centered
until the
very end.

The <H1 to H6> or Heading Tags

There are six basic heading tags. To the novice HTML user, the purpose of heading tags (<H1>, <H2>, <H3>, <H4>, <H5>, and <H6>) is to make text bigger or smaller — with the <H1> tag displaying the largest text and <H6> displaying the smallest text. (See Figures 2-1 and 2-2.) However, in reality, heading tags represent HTML's way of allowing a Webtop publisher to signal to the reader the levels of the document.

For example, you can think of headings as outlines. In an outline, the main topic is usually displayed with the most prominent heading at the top of the document. Less important information or subordinate topics are generally displayed later in the outline, in a less noticeable way.

Take this book for instance. It has at least six levels of headings:

\<H1\>   A first level heading is the name of the book \<H1\>.

\<H2\>   There are four sections in the book. Section headings are down one level of importance from the name of the book \<H2\>.

\<H3\>   Each section has several chapters. Chapter headings are subordinate or down another level of importance \<H3\>.

\<H4\>   The activity headings are subordinate or down to a fourth level of importance \<H4\>.

\<H5\>   Paragraph headings go down to the fifth subordinate level \<H5\>.

\<H6\>   Finally, the activity steps and text can be at the lowest heading level \<H6\>.

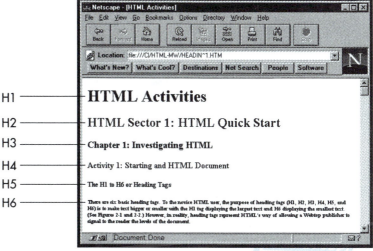

Figure 2-1
The Heading Tags — Before

Figure 2-2
The Heading Tags — After

On the Web, these levels are usually represented by the size of the text. For example, look how the tags are entered in Figure 2-1 and compare that with the result in the browser in Figure 2-2.

The Paragraph \<P\>, and Break \<BR\> Tags

Documents have breaks between paragraphs. There are two simple kinds of breaks you can use in an HTML document. They are:

- The **\<P\>** paragraph break tag. A paragraph break \<P\> tag adds an extra line between paragraphs. This would be like using a double-space command in your word processor.
- The **\<BR\>** break tag. The break tag is like using an Enter or Return key in a word processor. This tag creates a very different effect. The \<BR\> tag simply ends the line, leaving only a single space between the lines.

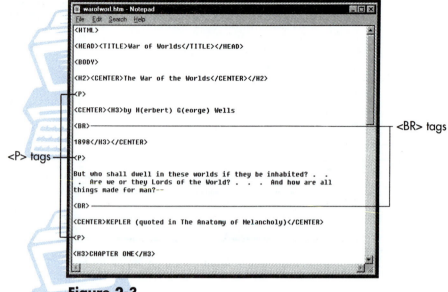

<P> tags

**
 tags**

Figure 2-3
The War of the Worlds[2]
Text and Tags

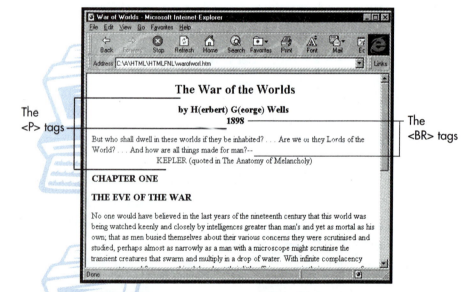

The
<P> tags

The
**
 tags**

Figure 2-4
The War of the Worlds
Displayed in Internet
Explorer

These two tags do not require close tags. In Figures 2-3 and 2-4, the <BR> and <P> tags are mixed to demonstrate how you may wish to use them in combination.

Your browser would display this text as shown in Figure 2-4.

Ordered <OL> and Unordered <UL> List <LI> Tags

Lists are easy in HTML. There are many kinds of lists you can create. This first kind of list is called an unordered list <UL>. *Unordered* simply means that the items in the list can be in any order. For example, if you were listing several animals at the zoo in no particular order you might put:

- Zebra
- Frog
- Aardvark

Unordered lists are usually marked by bullets (•). (See Figure 2-5 and the result in Figure 2-6.)

FAQs

Why do you never see close </BR> or close </P> tags?

Break tags are a little different than most other tags. Break tags aren't usually written as pairs. The open tag is usually sufficient to do the job.

[2]The Gutenberg Project: gopher://spinaltap.micro.umn.edu/11/Ebooks/

Ordered lists are used to show a sequence and are usually numbered accordingly. For example:

1. Start the car with your foot on the brake.

2. Put the car in gear.

3. Let off the brake slowly.

4. Press gently on the gas.

You can create as many items on your ordered or unordered lists as you wish. Each new item is set off by a list tag <LI> as shown in Figure 2-5.

Here is a list of Aesop's Fables in an unordered list format in a text editor.

The final result looks like Figure 2-6.

Ordered lists are constructed like unordered lists, only you substitute the ordered list tag <OL> for the unordered list tag <UL>. Your result will display numbers as shown in Figure 2-7.

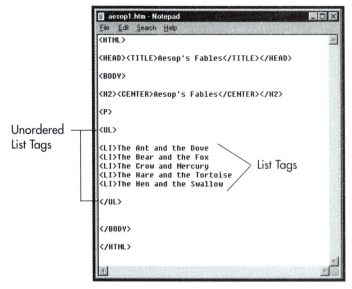

Figure 2-5
Creating an Unordered, or Bulleted, List

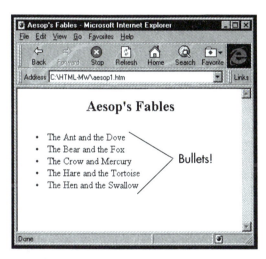

Figure 2-6
Aesop's Fables as an Unordered, or Bulleted, List.

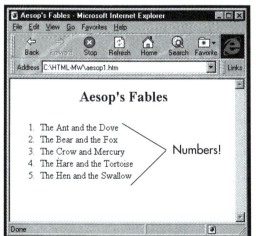

Figure 2-7
Aesop's Fables as a Numbered, or Enumerated, List.

FAQs

How can you easily change an unordered list to an ordered list in HTML?

f you have created an unordered list like:
<UL>
<LI>Item
<LI>Item
<LI>Item
</UL>

All you need to do to change your list to an ordered, or numbered, list is to change the <UL> to <OL>, as in:

<OL>
<LI>Item 1
<LI>Item 2
<LI>Item 3
</OL>

Digging Deeper into HTML Tags **27**

Debriefing

Review the Table of Tags displayed below. You will use these tags in the activities that follow. Try and memorize each tag.

Table of Tags for Chapter 2 and Activities 2 and 3		
Headings	<H1></H1> <H2></H2> <H3></H3> <H4></H4> <H5></H5> <H6></H6>	Heading tags make text appear larger or smaller depending on the number in the tag. <H1> allows the largest letters (or heading), while <H2> displays letters that are slightly smaller. The <H6> tag displays the smallest letters (or heading).
Paragraph Break (double-space)	<P>	This tag separates paragraphs by adding a line or a space. A closing tag </P> is optional.
Simple or Line Break (single space)	 	The tag creates a line break without adding an extra space between paragraphs.
Unordered List	<UL> <LI> <LI> <LI> </UL>	This sequence of tags creates bulleted lists, for example: • Something • Something • Something The UL is short for Unordered List. The LI tag means List.
Ordered List	<OL> <LI> <LI> <LI> </OL>	This sequence of tags creates numbered lists, for example: 1. Something 2. Something 3. Something The OL is short for Ordered List. The LI tag means List.
Center	<CENTER> </CENTER>	The <CENTER> tag centers the text in the browser window.

all Tags, Short Tags, and Tags that Make a List

In Chapter 2, you learned how formatting tags can add interest to your Webtop creations. In this activity, you will open your **act1.html** file and add formatting tags to your Web page.

Before you finish, make sure you save your Webtop file as **act2.html** or **act2.htm.** The **2** signifies that this is the HTML file for Activity **2.** You should then have two files in your HTML-?? folder (see Figure A2-2a):

- **act1.html** or **act1.htm**
- **act2.html** or **act2.htm**

Keep copies of all your work. If you accidentally destroy your **act2.html** file, you can always go back to your **act1.html** file and restore your work.

O b j e c t i v e s :

- Open your file **act1.html**.
- Save your Web document file as **act2.html**.
- Add paragraph, center, heading, list, and break tags.
- Save, test, and debug your Web document.

Step 1:

To open your Web page file:

1A: Open your text editor.

1B: Select **Open** from the **File** menu and open your Web page file **act1.html** as displayed in Figure A2-1a or Figure A2-1b.

Hint! Windows Notepad only looks for .txt (for Text) files. Notepad users have to change the option in the Open and Save As dialog boxes to include All Files (*.*) in order to uncover the .html or .htm file types.

Figure A2-1a
Open **act1.html** in Windows Notepad

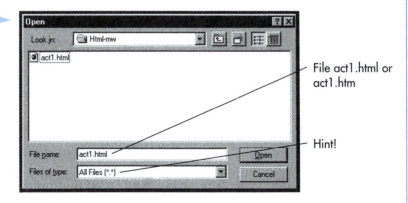

File act1.html or act1.htm

Hint!

Figure A2-1b
Open **act1.html** in
SimpleText

Step 2: Select **Save As** from the **File** pull-down menu. Save the new file as **act2.html** or **act2.htm**. (See Figure A2-2a or Figure A2-2b.)

Figure A2-2a
Save As dialog box in
Windows

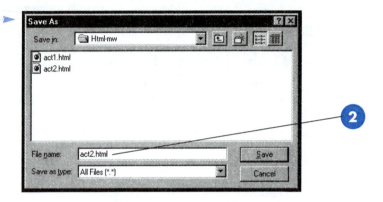

Figure A2-2b
Save As dialog box on a
Macintosh

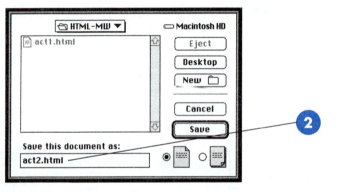

Note: If you are using a word processor, make sure you save your Web page as a text document file with the .htm or the .html extension.

Step 3: To center and enlarge your name:

3A: Enter the open tag <CENTER> before the word *Hi!* as shown in Figure A2-3. Enter the close tag </CENTER> after your name.

3B: Enter the open <H1> tag before the word *Hi!* as shown in Figure A2-3. Enter the close </H1> tag after your name in the first sentence.

3C: Enter a paragraph tag <P> to provide a space between your name and the sentence that describes where you live.

3D: Enter <H3> open and </H3> close tags around the remainder of the text.

3E: Enter <BR> tags after each sentence as marked in Figure A2-3.

Figure A2-3
Adding Interest to
act2.html
A - Enter <CENTER> tags
B - Enter <H1> tags
C - Enter <P> tag
D - Enter <H3> tags
E - Enter <BR> tags

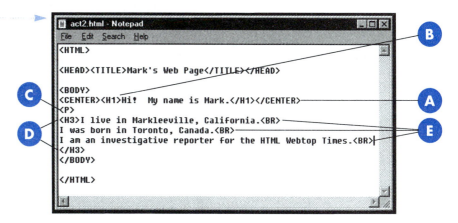

Hint! You can test your page as many times as you like during this activity by saving your file and opening the file in your Web browser. Review Activity 1, Steps 5 – 7 if you need help previewing your work in your browser. Remember to use the Reload or Refresh buttons if you change your Web page.

Step 4: To create an unordered list:

4A: Enter a <P> tag to leave a double space between the paragraph and the start of the list.

4B: Key the words *I like to:* as shown in Figure A2-4.

4C: Enter the unordered list tag <UL>.

4D: Enter five list tags <LI> followed by five things you like to do as shown in Figure A2-4.

4E: End the list with the close unordered list tag </UL>.

FAQs

What happens if I forget the slash?

othing. And that's a problem. If you forget the slash to end a </CENTER> command your browser continues to center ALL the text. Without the slash, your browser doesn't know when to stop. The net effect will be to start an HTML version of a run-away train, speeding along the tracks heading for disaster! Help stop HTML by using the </> to close your HTML commands.

Figure A2-4

Creating an Unordered List

A - Enter a <P> tag
B - Key *I like to:*
C - Enter the <UL> tag
D - Enter <LI> tags
E - Enter the </UL> tag

Step 5: Save and test your updated Web page. Return to Activity 1 if you have trouble saving and testing your page. Make any corrections that are necessary. Try the Reload or Refresh button to reload a corrected Web page. Your Web page should look similar to Figure A2-5.

Hint! Compare Figures A1-9b and A2-5 to see how the Web page was improved.

Figure A2-5

Web page **act2.html**

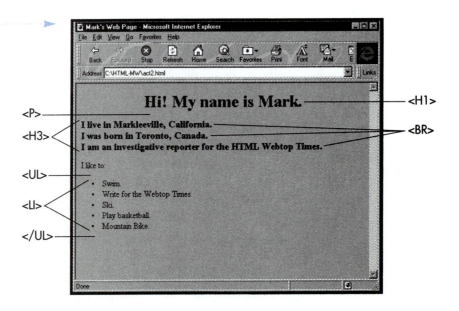

FAQs

Are HTML tags always <UPPERCASE>?

o. They can be <UPPERCASE> or <lowercase> or a <MixTure> of UPPER– and lowercase letters. Many professionals use <UPPERCASE> commands so they can see them easier. Others find that <lowercase> html commands allow them to see the text more easily. It is up to you.

Debriefing

You are beginning to learn how HTML works, but the best is yet to come. In the next chapter you will surf the Web looking for URLs or addresses for your hypertext links. Hypertext links are what makes the WWW interesting and better than many other forms of communication.

Remember the following as you continue to the next Webtop project:

1. Formatting tags add interest to simple Web pages.

2. The <CENTER></CENTER> tags centers the text when viewed in a Web browser.

3. The heading tags <H?> can be any size. <H1> displays the largest text format. <H6> displays the smallest text format. Don't forget to close heading tags </H?>.

4. The paragraph tag <P> divides text with a space. The break <BR> tags starts a new line without leaving a space.

5. Unordered lists are easy to create with the <UL><LI><LI><LI></UL> tags. Unordered lists usually display a bullet (•) before each item on the list.

6. Ordered lists are easy to create with the <OL><LI><LI><LI></OL> tags. Ordered lists display a number (1, 2, 3, etc.) before each item in the list.

Extension: For a little extra credit, return to your document act2.html and change the unordered bulleted list to a numbered, or ordered, list.

The Webtop Publishing Process

This activity helps you practice the HTML skills you have learned in Activities 1 and 2. For this project, you will use the five steps to the **Webtop Publishing Process** or **IPTCP**. The five steps include:

1. **Investigate** your topic.

2. **Plan** your Web page.

3. **Take a look around** for new ideas.

4. **Create** your Webtop publication.

5. **Publish** on the Web.

O b j e c t i v e s :

- Use the five-step Webtop Publishing Process.
- Create a Web page for a friend.
- Be creative in your Webtop publishing.

Step 1: Investigate your topic

Pick out someone from the local crowd. It may be a friend, a family member, community leader, or even your pet fish, cat, or dog. As an investigative reporter, you need to interview your "someone" and find out some basic information about them. Have them answer the following questions:

A. What is your first name?

B. Where do you live? (city, state/province/region, country only)

C. Where were you born?

D. What are your five favorite things to do?

E. What were your favorite three subjects in school in order of personal preference?

F. Who are the three people in history you admire most? Rank from number 1 to number 3.

Activity 3 Introducing Others to the Web

Write all of these details down on this official Mark Web notes page.

> **Step 2:** **Plan your Web page**

Take out a big piece of paper and plan out how you want your page to look in a Web browser.

Decide what size <H1–6> tags you are going to use and where. Decide which pieces of information you want to place in lists and how you want your lists to appear. Do you want bulleted lists or numbered lists?

> **Step 3:** **Take a look around for new ideas**

In Chapter 3, Activity 4, you will learn to surf the Web for new ideas on how to make your great Web pages even better. For now, borrow a few ideas from your friends and those in your class. If they know how to do something you don't know how to do, ask them to show you the techniques and tags they used. Look around for the coolest Web page ideas and make them your own.

> **Step 4:** **Create your Webtop publication**

Enter your starting tags and begin! Try to follow your plan. However, if you get a new idea, try it! Remember to save and test your Web page frequently. Use the following file name:

act3.html or **act3.htm**

Hint: Think about the resources you have that can save you time and effort on this project. For example, you already have the HTML starting tags entered in **act1.html**. You can simply open **act1.html** and save it as **act3.html**. This way you don't have to reenter your <HTML> starting tags. You may have to delete a little text, but that is easier than entering in all of those brackets!

> **Step 5:** **Publish on the Web**

There are two ways to view your documents:

Viewing and Publishing Locally: You can publish and view Web pages stored locally on your computer's hard drive, floppy disk, or on your local network file server. You are not yet on the Web, but you can create Web pages and test them just fine.

Viewing and Publishing on the Web: Many people think that if they create a Web page on their computer that everyone else can view it on the WWW. This is not the case. Before Web pages can be seen all over the world on the WWW, you need to save, or **post**, your Web pages on a special Web server. Web servers are special computers that have software that speaks the language of the Web (HTML). These special computers use a communications protocol known as HTTP. HTTP is an acronym for HyperText Transfer Protocol. HTTP is a special protocol that transfers HTML Web pages over the Net.

The machines that understand HTTP have special software that allow you to display your Web pages to the entire Web. Managing every Web HTTP server is a person who helps post pages on a Web server. This person is often called a Webmaster. Your Webmaster can show you what you must do to post your Web pages on a Web server. If you don't have access to a Web server yet, relax. We will give you more information about how Webmasters manage all those Web pages later on. For now, you can still view your Web page locally from your computer.

Debriefing

You can create all kinds of documents for the Web. Be creative and try a few new pages on your own. In the next activity, you will be able to visit my *HTML Activities Web Page*. From there you will be able to get all sorts of new ideas. Don't forget the five steps of the Webtop Publishing Process as you plan and create your new Web pages:

1. **Investigate** your topic.
2. **Plan** your Web page.
3. **Take a look around** for new ideas.
4. **Create** your Webtop publication.
5. **Publish** on the Web.

Chapter 3

Searching for Clues

The Web displays the infinite creativity of its Web page authors. There is a lot of creativity on the Web and the number of interesting Web pages is growing exponentially. Every second the clock ticks, someone is posting a new Web page on the Web.

Before continuing further, follow **Mark Web** as he takes you on a surfing trip for new Webtop publishing ideas. There are a million and one talented Web page authors, and a zillion good HTML ideas to find.

In Chapters 1 and 2, you learned how HTML tags work. You know how to spot pairs of tags, like <H1></H1>, and tags that work alone, like <BR>. In this chapter, you will learn some simple techniques that allow you to peek inside most Web pages. There you will find many, many ideas. And, by using Web search tools, you can pinpoint additional Web pages of personal interest with cool designs.

You will also learn how to spot other HTML tricks of the trade, like attributes and values. **Attributes** and **values** allow the Webtop publisher to define more precisely how a tag displays information in a Web browser.

O b j e c t i v e s :

- View HTML source codes on the Web.
- Use attributes and values in HTML tags.
- Discuss copyright issues on the Web.
- Locate Web page URLs and titles.
- Construct hypertext links.
- Insert graphics into Web pages.
- Enter lines into Web pages.
- Create enumerated and embedded lists.
- Change background color, link, and text colors.
- Use tags that add emphasis.

Uncovering the Hidden Truth!

"Back in the old days, grandpas the world over carried big, fat pocket watches. If you wanted to know how a clock worked, you just opened the back of the pocket watch and you could easily see what made it tick. It's the same with Web pages."

"Let me give you some inside tips on how to peek inside a Web page and view the hidden secrets that make the Web page tick."

- First, start your Web browser and start surfing. Keep a lookout for interesting Web pages. You may even want to use a Web search engine to narrow your search to topics of personal interest.
- Second, when you find a Web page you really like, open it up and peek inside and see what makes it work.

"Let me show you what I mean."

"This is one of my favorite Web pages. It's my personal Web page... no wonder I like it!" (See Figure 3-1.)

"To see inside a Web page, select the **View, Source** or the **View, Document Source** command. Wait a second, and zip! Up comes the Web page with all of its HTML tags showing. Take a good look at Figure 3-2."

- Look for any tags you have already learned.
- Identify the starting tags.
- Look for the heading tags.

"Now look for any new tags you might find. Do you see any strangely new tags?"

"Browsers use different names and different locations for the View Source feature."

- The Internet Explorer displays the **View**, **Source** command under the **View** menu. Click on **View** and select **Source** as displayed in Figure 3-3a. You can also click the right mouse key to see the View Source menu.
- Netscape also puts the feature under the **View** pull-down menu (see Figure 3-3b). Regardless of where it is located on your browser, the View Source feature lets you see ASCII HTML tags underneath the Web page as displayed in Figure 3-2."

Hint! You can also click your right mouse button on Internet Explorer for Windows and locate the View, Source command.

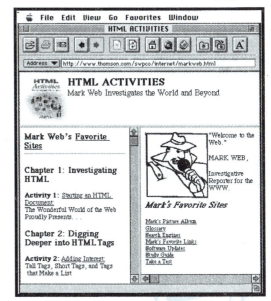

Figure 3-1:
The Mark Web Home Page on the Web

Figure 3-2:
The Mark Web Home Page from Deep Inside

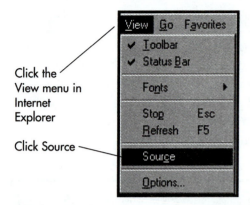

Click the
View menu in
Internet
Explorer

Click Source

Figure 3-3a
Internet Explorer's View
Source Command

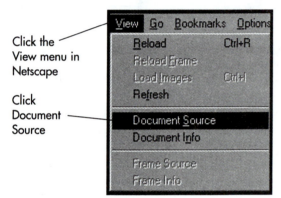

Click the
View menu in
Netscape

Click
Document
Source

Figure 3-3b
Netscape's View Source
Command

FAQs

**What is the
difference between
a Web page, a
home page, and a
Web document?**

...one that we
can tell. They all
mean fairly much the
same thing — that is,
a text file that uses
HTML tags that a Web
browser can read.

Attributes and Values < = >

Many of the strangely different tags you see on the Web use attributes and values. **Attributes** describe in detail what the tag is meant to display. Attributes include words like BGCOLOR, ALIGN, or HREF.

There are many examples of how **values** are used. You can often spot a value by the equal (=) sign. For example, here is how a <BODY> tag uses a value to change the background color on a Web page to the color green.

<BODY BGCOLOR=#00FF00>

Trust me. 00FF00 really is green. Just ask any computer. The number (yes, it is a number) 00FF00 stands for green in the hexadecimal numbering system. Hexadecimal (HEX for short) is a numbering system based on 16 rather than 10. The letters A, B, C, D, E, and F are added to the numbers 0, 1, 2, 3, 4, 5, 6, 7, 8, and 9 to create all sorts of new combinations. Here are the basic colors in hexadecimal:

White	FFFFFF
Black	000000
Red	FF0000
Blue	0000FF
Green	00FF00

Shades of these primary colors are created by changing the numbers. For example, a really cool sky blue can be created by entering 00CCFF. Do you want yellow? Try FFFF00. A nice light purple? Try FF95FF. (Now, you could be conventional and key in the words RED, or WHITE, as in BGCOLOR=RED, but that takes all the suspense out of the hexidecimal color system!)

Before we got lost in the hexidecimal color values, we were making a point about attributes and values. Attributes and values create exciting and interesting changes in a Web page. However, you must use them expertly.

For example, if you insert BGCOLOR=#AAFF00 in the body tag as marked in Figure 3-4, you end up with a really ugly slime green color as the background of your Web page. If you add the attribute TEXT and assign the value =#D38800, your text turns to an ugly orange. You are now well on your way to the ugliest Web page in cyberspace. (There are cyberlaws against using such ugly color combinations!)

Values and attributes work with lots of tags, as you will see, and they can change more than background or link colors.

Grabbing a Graphic with <IMG SRC>

Another thing you will notice as you surf the Web (looking for answers to the mysteries of HTML) is that nearly all the home pages have some sort of picture or graphic.

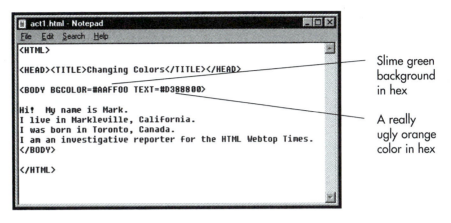

```
act1.html - Notepad
File  Edit  Search  Help
<HTML>

<HEAD><TITLE>Changing Colors</TITLE></HEAD>

<BODY BGCOLOR=#AAFF00 TEXT=#D38800>

Hi!  My name is Mark.
I live in Markleville, California.
I was born in Toronto, Canada.
I am an investigative reporter for the HTML Webtop Times.
</BODY>

</HTML>
```

Slime green background in hex

A really ugly orange color in hex

Figure 3-4
Creating a Background Color

If you look inside my Web page you may notice the graphic in Figure 3-5, the picture of me reporting. Why don't you grab it? You can, you know. It's easy if you understand the secret code.

Graphics are identified by addresses the same way Web pages are. They are not physically connected to your Web page. They must be added or loaded upon request.

The tag <IMG SRC>, which is short for IMaGe SeaRCh, searches for graphics and inserts them in the place defined by the attributes and values you put in. In Activity 7, you will learn three ways to grab this graphic. To do so, you need to know where it is located. On my Web page, the graphics are located at the following address:

A nice likeness, don't you think?

Figure 3-5
A Graphic

http://www.thomson.com/swpco/internet/markweb.html

Knowing what all the slashes mean helps you understand this secret code. The slashes let you know that you are in a new folder or directory. In this case, the path to my pictures looks like this:

http://	=	Hypertext Transfer Protocol
www.thomson.com	=	The computer where the picture is found
/swpco	=	The SWPCO folder or directory
/internet	=	The Internet sub folder or subdirectory
/markweb.html	=	My Web page file (every investigative reporter should have one)

Once you find the Web page, click on the link called *Mark's Picture Album*.

Copyright Issues

There are two kinds of graphics on the Web:

• Those you can take off the Web and use on your Web page.
• Those you can't take off the Web.

Copyright law protects artistic work, characters (like cartoons), logos and trademarks, and written works from theft or misuse by

FAQs

Do I need to include the # sign before the color number attributes?

Early browsers required a # sign before the number of the color. Now, the number alone is all that is required. In other words, =ffffff is interpreted the same as =#ffffff. In fact, for some colors you don't even need to know the number. The value =white will work along with most other primary colors: =red, =blue, and =yellow.

FAQs

What is a .gif file?

A .gif file is a type of graphics file format. The letters .gif are short for Graphics Interchange Format. GIF is pronounced "jiff" in some areas and "giff" in others. GIF files transfer quickly over the Web, so they became popular. Many early browsers only support-ed .gif files. The format itself is owned by CompuServe. There have been some copy-right issues emerge over the use of this CompuServe format, so many have started to use the JPEG format. (See FAQs: What is a .jpg file?)

FAQs

What is a .jpg file?

A .jpeg or .jpg file is short for Joint Photographic Expert Group format. The format is a public standard established by an international committee. JPEG (pronounced "J-peg") files are appearing on the Web with more and more frequency. This open standard is read by any quality browser.

unauthorized individuals. For example, Coke, Pepsi, Disney, and ESPN all have copyright to their pictures, logos, images, and graphics. Copyright law applies to books, magazines, newspapers, and other forms of communication, including radio and television. For example:

- When you watch a rented video you will see the FBI statement warning you against copying the video.
- When you open a book you can see the trademarks and copyright pages in the front of the book.
- When you watch a professional football game, the announcer will say, "Any use of this broadcast without the express written permission of the NFL, the Oakland Raiders, and the Cincinnati Bengals is prohibited."

Copyright exists on the Web as well. When you use a picture on your Web page that belongs to someone else, you could be violating copyright law.

To help keep you out of jail, I have placed pictures of me on my Web page that you can use to experiment with. You will learn how to down-load these pictures to your HTML-?? folder in Activity 9. A word of caution is in order: Only download the pictures you intend to use. Graphics can take up a lot of memory on your computer's hard drive.

As a user of this book, there are no copyright restrictions to using the graphics from my Web page. Use them if you wish.

On the *HTML Activities Web Page* there are also links to other Web pages where you can borrow graphics free of charge without breaking copyright restrictions.

Debriefing

Here are the notes for this chapter:

1. To see inside a Web page, select the **View**, **Source** or **View**, **Document Source** command on your Web browser.

2. When you are looking at Web pages for new HTML tags and commands, keep an eye out for attributes and values. Attributes describe what a tag is meant to display, like <BGCOLOR>. A value indicates the degree of change. For example, a color value can be changed from FFFFFF for white to FF0000 for red.

3. Graphics are easy to copy from the Web. Use the <IMG SRC> tag to insert graphics into your Web page.

4. Don't take a graphic that doesn't belong to you or that is copy-righted. There are many graphics available on the Web at no charge, so it doesn't pay to steal any.

5. The two most popular graphics file formats on the Web are .gif and .jpg (or .jpeg).

Hyperlinks in Hyperspace

Surf's up. It is time to find some Web pages to which you would like to hyperlink from your own personal Web page.

The purpose of this activity is to find and record ten Webtop **URLs** and **titles**. That's right! A URL is a Uniform Resource Locator, which is a fancy way of saying a Web address. URLs help you find other pages on the WWW. You can see URLs in the location or status windows on your browser (See Figure A4-2).

The title of a Web page is found in the Title bar of your browser as seen in Figure A4-2. Create a table like the one below. Record 10 URLs you wish to use as you create hypertext links in Activity 5. We have listed five URLs for you on the *HTML Activities Web Page*. From there, you can surf for five more URLs to complete your list. The Disney Web page (#0) provides an example of how to fill out this table. (Be sure to use a separate sheet of paper.)

Activity 4 Table of URLs "Ten Sites Worth Visiting"	
URL	**Title**
0: http://www.disney.com	The Disney Web Page
1: http://	
2: http://	
3: http://	
4: http://	
5: http://	
6: http://	
7: http://	
8: http://	
9: http://	
10: http://	

O b j e c t i v e s :

- Open your Web browser.
- Find the *HTML Activities Web Page.*
- Locate and record ten really cool Web pages.

"The following steps are intended to help those with little or no Web experience. If you are already a Web wizard, skip to Step 4C and zip right to my Web page. If you are a beginner, start with Step 1 and follow the steps one-by-one. I will meet you at my Web page."

> **Step 1:** Start your Web browser by double-clicking on a browser icon as shown in Figures A4-1a and A4-1b.

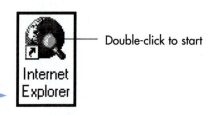

Double-click to start

Figure A4-1a
The Internet Explorer Icon

Figure A4-1b
The Netscape Icon

Double-click to start

> **Step 2:** Explore the first Web page you see (called your beginning Web page).
>
> **2A:** Use the scroll bars to move down your beginning Web page.
>
> **2B:** Look for hypertext links. Look for words that are <u>underlined</u> and appear in a *different color*. (See Figure A4-2.)

Figure A4-2
Hypertext Links
A - Scroll bar
B - Hyptertext link

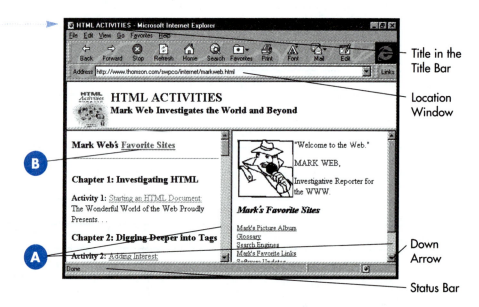

FAQs

How Many Web pages are on the WWW?

No one knows. Perhaps billions and billions. If you select 100 new hyperlinks a day every day for 100 years you can only view 3,650,000 Web pages, a tiny fraction of the possible Web pages on the Web.

2C: Click on any hypertext link you see. You will be taken to a new Web page.

2D: Click on another hypertext link. It doesn't matter which one you select, just click, and click, and click. You will be taken to another Web page, and another, and another. Stop clicking when your hand gets tired. Congratulations! You have just surfed the WWW.

Step 3: Use the Back Button, the Forward Button, and the Home button as shown in Figures A4-3a and A4-3b:

Figure A4-3a
Internet Explorer Toolbar Buttons
A - Back button
B - Forward button
C - Home button

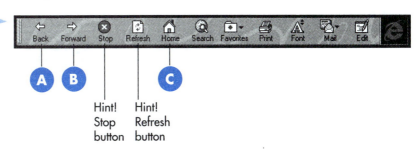

Figure A4-3b
Netscape Toolbar Buttons
A - Back button
B - Forward button
C - Home button

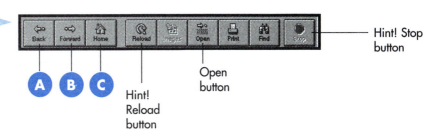

3A: Use the **Back** button to move back several Web pages.

3B: Use the **Forward** button to move forward a few Web pages.

3C: Use the **Home** button to return to your beginning Web page.

Hint! If a Web page doesn't come in "normally" try the Reload or Refresh button. If a Web page takes too long to load or appear, click on the Stop button and try again later.

Step 4: To enter the URL for the *HTML Activities Web Page*:

4A: Select **Open**, or **Open Location** from the **File** pull-down menu. **Note:** You may also click the Open button as shown in Figure A4-3b.

Hint! Some browsers use the command Open URL.

4B: Enter the following URL for the *HTML Activities Web Page* in the entry box. (See Figures A4-4a and A4-4b.)

http://www.thomson.com/swpco/internet/markweb.html

Note: A word of caution — you must enter the URL exactly as shown. If one letter is incorrect, you might end up anywhere. Also remember that there are no spaces in a URL.

Hint! The http:// is optional on most browsers, so you don't usually have to type it.

4C: Click **Open** or **OK**.

Figure A4-4a
Internet Explorer:
The URL for the *HTML Activities Web Page*
C - Enter the URL
D - Click OK

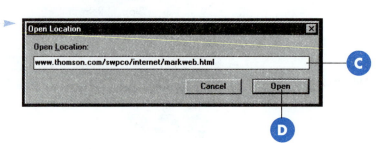

Figure A4-4b
Netscape:
The URL for the *HTML Activities Web Page*
C - Enter the URL
D - Click Open

4D: Use the Down arrow (see Figure A4-2) to scroll down the *HTML Activities Web Page* and click on Activity 4.

Hint! You may want to put the *HTML Activities Web Page* in your Bookmark or Favorites list. A Bookmark or Favorites list is a way your browser has of remembering your favorite Web pages. Different browsers create these lists in slightly different ways. For example, to create a Bookmark in Netscape, select **Add Bookmark** from the **Bookmarks** pull-down menu. The Internet Explorer uses the **Add to Favorites** command under the **Favorites** menu.

Note: All of the URLs used in this book are found on the *HTML Activities Web Page*. URLs are constantly changing on the World Wide Web. As URLs change, updates are being made to the *HTML Activities Web Page* for your convenience. You may want to Bookmark this Web page while you are taking the course.

Step 5: To find five URLs and links to other great Webtop publishing sites:

5A: Select the Activity 4 link on the *HTML Activities Web Page*.

5B: Try the five URLs on the list. If you like them, write down the title from the title bar (as marked in Figure A4-2) and add the URL and the title to your list. Each page can take you to new places as well. Record your list of 10 total URLs and titles. (You will need this list in Activity 5.)

Step 6: Exit your browser.

Debriefing

Using a browser is easy. You now have conquered the skills of starting your browser, using hypertext or hyperlinks, and entering URLs to find a specific Web page.

The *HTML Activities Web Page* will help you find the sites that are used in this text, and other sites with fantastic Webtop publications. Bookmark this Web page for future reference.

In the activities that follow, you will search for more on-line Webtop publications that you can use to gather ideas and to learn more about the wonderful on-line publishing playground called the WWW.

The best way to "peek inside" and see how a Web page was created is to use the **View Source** command on your browser. Viewing and thinking about how someone else has created a great-looking page can help you invent new ways of creating great Webtop publications yourself.

Extension: For a little extra credit, view the HTML source code for each of the 10 Web pages you have listed.

Go to each of the Web pages you have recorded in your chart and select the **View Source** command. In Netscape, select **View Source** from the **View** menu (Figure 3-3b). In Internet Explorer, click **View**, then click **Source** from the pull-down menu (Figure 3-3a).

Look for new ideas and tags that are new to you. Record on a separate sheet of paper 10 new HTML tags that should go in the chart below.

New Tag	Guess: "What does this tag do?"

Hyper-flight to Anywhere

In Activities 1 and 2, you learned how to use HTML starting and formatting tags. In this activity, you will add hyperlink tags to your Web pages. Hyperlink tags allow you to create interactive links to other Web pages. So, dust off your "Ten Sites Worth Visiting" from the Activity 4 Table of URLs. You will need the Titles and URLs you recorded to complete Step 3.

While we are on the subject of hyperlinks, a slight distinction can be made between **hyperlinks** and **hypertext links**:

- Hypertext links are words that you can click that link you to other Web pages, pictures, and graphics.
- Hyperlinks can be pictures, called icons, that you can click. Hyperlinks can also take you to other Web pages, pictures, and graphics.

Later we will show you how to make hyperlinks out of graphic images. In this activity, we will work with words and create hypertext links. You will create two kinds of hypertext links:

- Hypertext links in a sentence or paragraph
- Hypertext links in a list

<A>Anchors</A> and Hypertext References (HREF="")

To create a hypertext link, you must use the HTML anchor tags. All hypertext links are marked by open and close anchor tags which look like this:

<A></A>

Think of these tags as a ship anchor with a long rope attached. The anchor attaches itself firmly to your Web page and the virtual anchor rope strings across the Web and attaches itself to Web pages, pulling them into your Web browser so you can view their contents.

Unlike the tags you have already learned, the <A></A> tags use some extra features that help locate new Web pages. To create hypertext links, you need to add attributes to the anchor tags. The key attribute is the Hypertext REFerence command or HREF. The HREF attribute is followed by an equal (=) sign and a value. The value, usually a URL, is identified between quotation marks ("") as in Figure A5-1.

The entire command will look like:

<A HREF="http://www.disney.com">The Disney Web Page</A>

Notice Figure A5-1. Between the <A></A> anchor open and close tags you can place words or text like "The Disney Web Page." The text between the tags will appear underlined and in a different color, as displayed in Figure A5-2.

Let's examine the parts of a hypertext link in Figures A5-1 and A5-2:

A: The open anchor tag

B: The HREF command

C: The equal (=) sign and the destination URL in quotation marks ("").

D: The title or a short descriptive statement about the Web page being requested. (This is the part that is seen on the Web page (See Figure A5-2).

E: The close anchor tag.

Figure A5-1
A Hypertext Link in HTML
A - The open Anchor tag
B - The HREF command
C - The equal (=) sign
and the URL in quotation
marks ("").
D - The title text
E - The close anchor tag.

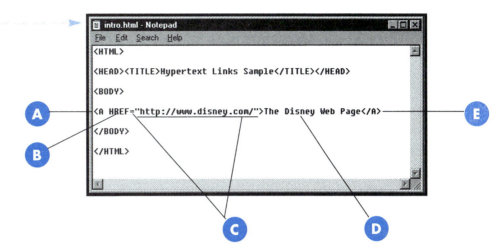

Figure A5-2
Hypertext Links Appear
Underlined and in a
Different Color

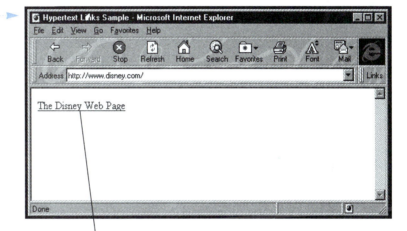

The title text appears underlined and in a different color

Table of Tags for Activity 5		
Anchor	<A></A>	The anchor tag. Used to create hypertext references.
Hypertext Reference	HREF=""	Hypertext REFerence. Used to indicate which URL, or Uniform Resource Locator, is being searched.

O b j e c t i v e s :

- Open your file **act2.html**.
- Save your Web document file as **act5.html**.
- Add hypertext links to your text.
- Save your work.
- Test your Web document's hypertext links in your browser.

Step 1: To open your Web page file:

1A: Open your text editor.

1B: Select **Open** from the **File** menu and open your Web page file **act2.html** (or **act2.htm** in Windows 3.1).

1C: Save your file with a new name, such as **act5.html**. (If you are using a word processor, make sure you save your Web page as a text file.)

Step 2: To create a list of hypertext links:

2A: Move your cursor below your unordered list and add a <P> tag as shown in Figure A5-3.

2B: Create a level 2 heading as shown below:

<H2>Ten Web Pages Worth Visiting</H2>

2C: Enter another paragraph tag: <P>

2D: Start your list with the Unordered List tag: <UL>

2E: Enter ten list tags: <LI> followed by hypertext anchor tags and attributes <A HREF=""></A> as shown below and in Figure A5-3:

<LI><A HREF=""></A>

Hint! Save time by using the copy and paste feature. Enter a single <LI><A HREF=""></A> string of tags, then copy it nine times. (You can also use the quick keys: In Windows, use Ctrl + C to copy and Ctrl + V to paste. On the Macintosh, use the Apple Key + C to copy and the Apple Key + V to paste.)

2F: Close the list with the unordered list tag </UL>.

FAQs

What is http://?

TTP is an acronym taken from the words HyperText Transfer Protocol. This protocol is the language the Web uses to transport Web pages around the world at lightening speed.

Figure A5-3
Creating Hypertext Links
A - Enter <P>
B - Enter <H2> tags
C - Enter <P>
D - Enter <UL>
E - Key <LI> <A
HREF=""></A>
F - Enter </UL>

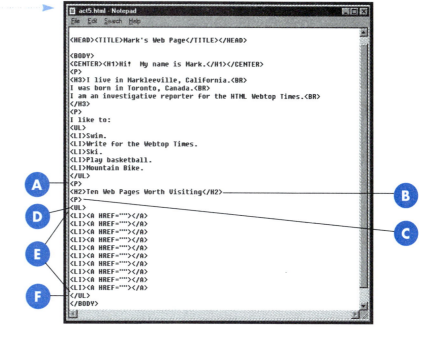

Step 3: Locate the URLs and Titles you recorded in Activity 4. Enter the URLs between the quotation marks (""), and the Titles between the >brackets< exactly as shown below and exactly as shown in Figure A5-4:

<LI><A HREF="http://www.disney.com">The Disney Web Page</A>

Figure A5-4
Enter URLs between the
quotation marks ("")

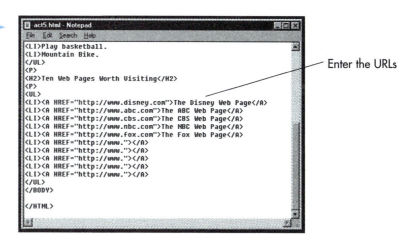

Enter the URLs

Note: URLs are case sensitive. That is, if the URL is written http://www.disney.com, you can't enter it as HTTP://WWW.Disney.Com.

Step 4: Test your Web page in your browser. (See Figure A5-5.) If you are connected to the Internet, you can try the links. They should take you to the Web page URLs you entered. If the links don't work, go back to the text editor file **act5.html** and fix the problems. It is rare that all the links in a Web page work correctly the first time.

Figure A5-5:
Test Your Links

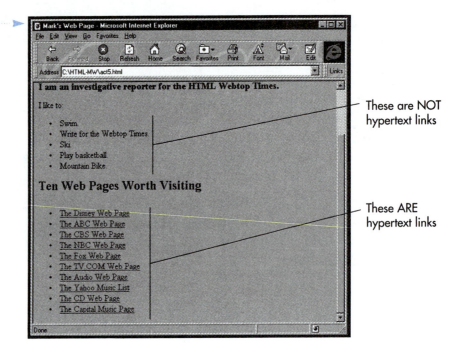

These are NOT hypertext links

These ARE hypertext links

Notes: If you don't have an Internet or Web connection, you will not be able to test your hypertext links.

Remember to save **act5.html** as a text file with .html as the extension. Windows 3.1 or DOS computers are going to require the .htm extension.

Step 5: Remember to save your work. Close and exit your browser and text editor.

Debriefing

Hypertext and hyperlinks are the tools that make HTML so powerful. Links are what makes the WWW exciting and interactive.

Creating a hypertext link is as easy as keying in the tag:

<A HREF="List URL"> List Title </A>

In this activity, you created hypertext links in a list. In the next activity, you will create links in a paragraph.

Extension: For extra credit, go to the Web and search (perhaps with a search engine) five links about business, government, or some other topic. Rank each item in the list from the most to least important. Make an ordered <OL> list. Make the most important link number 1 and the least important number 5 in the list.

A Hyper-flight Back Home

Now that you have mastered hypertext links in a list, it is time to insert them into a paragraph. Hypertext links in a paragraph are extremely valuable for creating reports, or explaining details to others over the Web.

Web paragraphs are usually short and to the point. Added explanations, or detail, is usually saved for additional Web pages you link to from the hypertext links in your paragraphs.

Links appear as <u>underlined</u> words in paragraphs. There is an example to follow in Figures A6-1 and A6-2.

O b j e c t i v e s :

- Visit various Web sites that list hypertext links for countries, cities, and towns.
- Record URLs for Web pages from the country, province or state, and city where you live.
- Record URLs for three cities you would like to visit.
- Record three additional URLs of interest.
- Write several short paragraphs about yourself embedding URLs you have recorded.

> **Step 1:**

To search for cities, towns, states, provinces, and countries:

1A: Go to the *HTML Activities Web Page* and select Activity 5. Click on one of the following links:

http://usacitylink.com/visitcity.html/

http://www.city.net/

http://www.city.com/

1B: Find the country, state/province/county, and city nearest to where you were born. On a separate sheet of paper record the URLs and the titles.

	URL	Titles
Country		
State/Province/County		
City or Town		

1C: Find three cities you would like to visit. Record the URLs.

Name of City	URL	Titles

1D: Find any additional sites or places you would like to visit or mention in your paragraph. You may have a URL for your school's Web page, or the Web page of a company you work for.

	URL	Titles
School Web Page		
Business Web Page		
Other Interesting Page		

Step 2:   Open your Web page file **act5.html** or **act5.htm** in your text editor. Save a new copy of the file as **act6.html** or **act6.htm**.

Step 3:   To insert hypertext links in a paragraph:

3A: Write a short paragraph called **About Me**. Use <H2> tags to create a heading for your paragraph as marked in Figure A6-1.

3B: Include the names of the three places you have recorded in Step 1B.

3C: Create hypertext links for three of the states, countries, or other places you found in Step 1B. Be sure to include your anchor, reference, and close anchor tags for each link as marked in Figure A6-1.

Note: If you have trouble remembering how to enter hypertext links, review Activity 5.

Figure A6-1

Hypertext Links in a
Paragraph
A - About Me paragraph
heading
B - Places
C - Hypertext links for
places in B

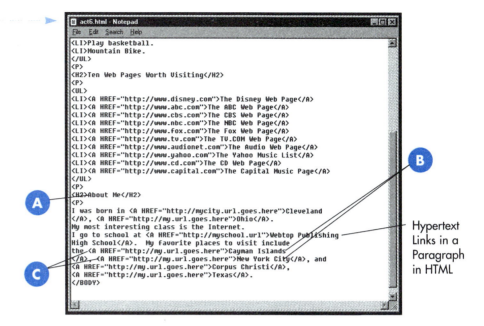

Hypertext
Links in a
Paragraph
in HTML

3D: View your new paragraph in your Web browser. The sample
paragraph looks like Figure A6-2 when it is displayed.

Figure A6-2

The Resulting Display of
Hypertext Links in a
Paragraph

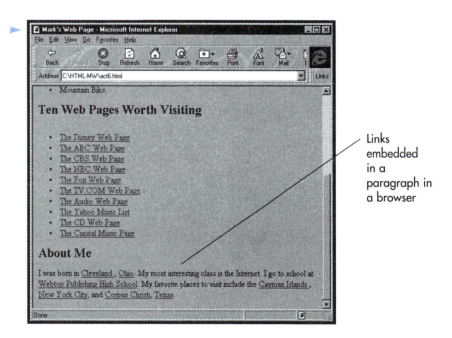

Links
embedded
in a
paragraph in
a browser

Hint! Make sure you include extra spaces before the anchor tags so the
paragraph looks correct when it is displayed. Don't include any extra
spaces where they are not necessary. You may have to display your paragraph in your browser and see where the spaces go, and what spaces
have been left out.

Step 4: Create another paragraph listing three cities you would like to visit as recorded in Step 1C. Label this paragraph **Places to Visit**. Use <H2> tags to mark the heading. Create three hypertext links inside this new paragraph.

Step 5: Create a final paragraph that discusses your school, a business or other interesting Web page as recorded in Step 1D. Label this paragraph with a title of your choice and mark it with the <H2> tag.

Step 6: Test, edit, and correct your paragraphs and links.

Step 7: When you are finished, resave your Web page as **act6.html** or **act6.htm**.

Step 8: Close or exit your browser.

Debriefing

Hypertext links put the fun into the Web. The links are what made the Web first become popular. Hypertext links represented a new way to share information around the world.

Cleaning up your paragraph: There are some guidelines that expert Webtop publishers use as they organize their paragraphs:

- Always provide spaces after commas, periods, and other punctuation marks.
- Place punctuation outside the anchor tags or after the anchor close tag.

Extension: DON'T LOOK AT THE HTML SAMPLE SHOWN BELOW! Find a partner first and prepare for a contest of HTML skill!

Both you and your partner have 60 seconds to find as many mistakes in the HTML Web page below as you can. Each of you must write down as many mistakes as you can find in 60 seconds. The one who finds the most mistakes wins! There are lots of errors! Can you find 10 or 15 of them?

```
<HTML><HEAD>
<TITLE>My Web Page<HEAD>
<P>
<H2>About Me</H1>
<PR>
I was <HR>born in <A HREF="http://cleveland.net">Cleveland,
<A> <B HREF="http://www.ohio.com">Ohio.</A>
My most interesting class is the Internet.I go to school at <A
HREF="http://www.wtphs.edu">Webtop Publishing
High School.</A>My favorite places to visit include
the <A HREF="http://cayman vacations.com">Cayman Islands
</A>, <A HREF="http://www.ny ny.gov">New York City</A>, and
<A HREF="http://www.corpuschristi.gov">Corpus Christi</A>,
<A HERF="http://www.texas.us"<Texas</A>.
</body>
```

traighten it out!

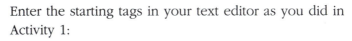
 | Add horizontal lines to a Web page.
• Add an ordered list to a Web page.
• Add emphasis to words on a Web page using various HTML formatting tags.

 traighten it out!

Web pages can get very long and very unorganized. However, there are many tags you can use to organize and format a Web page. For example, you can bold or italicize certain words. You can also add lines to separate various parts of your Web page document. Here are some new tags to use in this activity:

Table of Tags for Activity 7		
Horizontal Rule	<HR>	Create horizontal lines
Bold	<B>	Bold text
Italics	<I>	Italicize text
Emphasis	<EM>	Emphasize text (often italics)
Strong Emphasis	<STRONG>	Strongly emphasize text (often bold)

O b j e c t i v e s :

- Add horizontal lines to a Web page.
- Add an ordered list to a Web page.
- Add emphasis to words on a Web page using various HTML formatting tags.

 Step 1: Enter the starting tags in your text editor as you did in Activity 1:

```
<HTML>
<HEAD><TITLE></TITLE></HEAD>
<BODY>
</BODY>
</HTML>
```

Step 2: Enter *Famous Quotes* between the <TITLE> tags.

Step 3: Type the following quotes and their authors between the <BODY> tags as they appear below:

Sir Winston Spencer Churchill

"Never give in, never give in, never, never, never — in nothing, great or small, large or petty — never give in except to the convictions of honor and good sense."

"Let us therefore brace ourselves to our duty, and so bear ourselves that, if the British Empire and its Commonwealth lasts for a thousand years, men will still say, this was their finest hour."

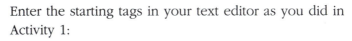

Activity **7**

Lines and Emphasis

Martin Luther King

"I say to you today, my friends, that in spite of the difficulties and frustrations of the moment I still have a dream. It is a dream deeply rooted in the American dream."

"I have a dream that one day this nation will rise up and live out the true meaning of its creed: "We hold these truths to be self-evident; that all men are created equal.""

"I have a dream that my four little children will one day live in a nation where they will not be judged by the color of their skin but by the content of their character.""

Mother Teresa of Calcutta

"Unless life is lived for others, it isn't worthwhile."

"As I often say to people who tell me they would like to serve the poor as I do, "What I can do, you cannot. What you can do, I cannot. But together we can do something beautiful for God.""

Step 4:   To organize the quotes:

4A: Separate each person being quoted with a horizontal rule <HR> tag as shown in Figure A7-1.

4B: Place <P> tags between each famous person and his or her quotes.

4C: Place <BR> tags to separate the paragraphs as marked in Figure A7-1.

4D: Center the name of each famous person with the <CENTER> </CENTER> tags.

4E: Make each famous person a level 2 heading by using the <H2></H2> heading tags.

Figure A7-1
Famous Quotes Web
Page Text and Tags
A - Enter <HR> tags
B - Enter <P> tags
C - Enter <BR> tags
D - Enter <CENTER> tags
E - Enter <H2> tags

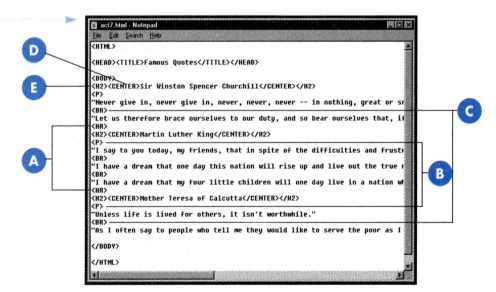

> **Step 5:** Save your new Web page as **act7.html**.

> **Step 6:** View your new Famous Quotes Web page in your browser. It should look similar to Figure A7-2.

Figure A7-2
Famous Quotes Displayed
In Your Browser
A - <HR>
B - <P>
C -
D - <CENTER>
E - <H2>

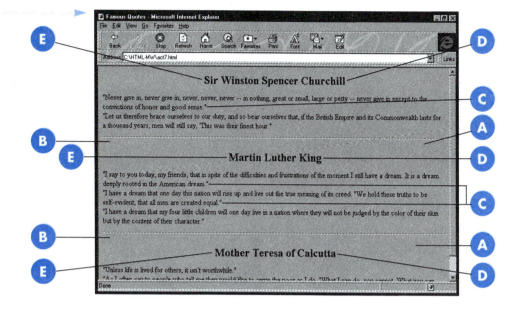

Be Creative with Additional Emphasis Tags: <B>, <I>, <EM>, and <STRONG>

There are many, many tags you can use to add emphasis to your Webtop words. Which ones you use are a matter of personal preference and choice. EXPERIMENT! Use some of these emphasis tags and see how they make the page look:

<B>Bold </B>
<I>Italics </I>
<EM>Emphasis </EM>
<STRONG>Stronger Emphasis </STRONG>

> **Step 7:** Be creative. Add interest to your Famous Quotes page by using the emphasis tags listed above. Experiment with each of these tags. You can emphasis certain words or sentences, or make each quote a little different. Play with the new tags. Remember, you can always delete tags that don't work.

Here is a sample:

Figure A7-3
Emphasis Tags in HTML

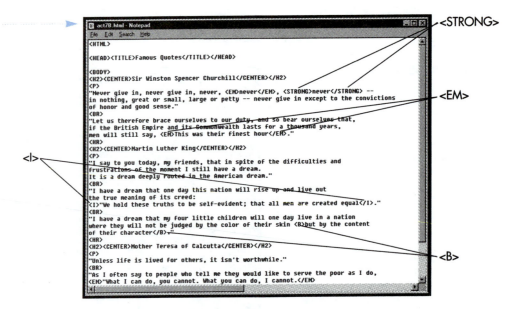

<STRONG>
<EM>
<I>
<B>

Figure A7-4
Result of Emphasis Tags
Displayed in a Browser

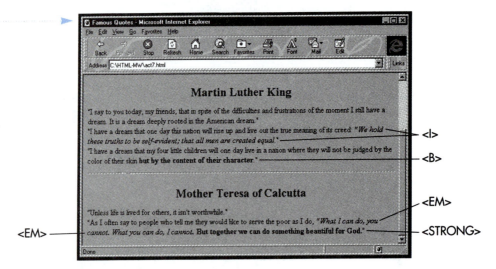

<I>
<B>
<EM>
<EM>
<STRONG>

Debriefing

Tags can organize and add interest to a Web page. The key is to use these formatting tags to add to the power of the words being used, not to detract from the words. You can easily overuse these kinds of tags. For example, the <BLINK> tag can really add emphasis, but may not be appropriate for certain kinds of quotes or words. Try using the <BLINK> tag in your page and see what I mean.

<BLINK>Sir Winston Spencer Churchill</BLINK>

When would it be good to use the <BLINK> tag for emphasis? Some people say, "Never!" What do you think?

ight it up!

Here's a chance for you to add some color to your Web pages. Creating colors also requires tags. There are three parts to a color tag:

1. The tag itself, like **<BODY>**.

2. An attribute — for example, if you want to change the background color in the body tag, you would add the attribute **bgcolor**, like this: <body bgcolor>.

3. A value — a value can be a number or a word. For example, you can change the background colors by using the following numbers or words to create a colored background.

Table of Tags for Activity 8

Red	=Red or =ff0000	Color value for red
Green	=Green or =00ff00	Color value for green
Blue	=Blue or =0000ff	Color value for blue
White	=White or =ffffff	Color value for white
Black	=Black or =000000	Color value for black
Background Color	bgcolor	The Background Color attribute
Link Color	link	The Hypertext & Hyperlink Color attribute
Visited Link Color	vlink	The Visited Hypertext & Hyperlink attribute
Text Color	text	The Text Color attribute

O b j e c t i v e s :

- Change the body background color of your Web page.
- Alter the link color of your Web page.
- Vary the visited link color of your Web page.
- Modify the text color in your Web page.

Step 1: Start your Web browser and your text editor.

Step 2: Open your personal Web page text document called **act6.htm** or **act6.html**.

Step 3: Find your open body tag <BODY> and:

3A: Insert the background color attribute **bgcolor** as shown in Figure A8-1a or A8-1b: <body **bgcolor**

3B: Insert an equal sign, followed by the name of a color or its numerical value: <body **bgcolor=blue** or <body **bgcolor=0000ff**.

> **Note:** Older browsers required a # sign after the = sign: <body **bgcolor =#0000ff**.

3C: Add a link attribute by entering the word **link=** after your color value as written here: **link=red** or **link= ff0000**. This will change the color of your hypertext links.

3D: Add a visited link attribute by using the **vlink=** attribute. A **visited link** is one you have already clicked on and visited. For example, if you change the visited link color to green, you can use either: **vlink=green** or **vlink=00ff00** as shown in Figure A8-1.

> **Hint!** Be sure not to make your link, visited link, or text colors the same color as your background. To do so would be to make the links or text disappear!

3E: Use the attribute **text=** to change the color of your words as they appear on the page. For example, to turn the text white, use either **text=white** or **text=ffffff**.

> **Hint!** All your changes will look something like this: <BODY BGCOLOR=BLUE LINK=RED VLINK=GREEN TEXT=WHITE> or if you use the hexadecimal numbering system, your changes will look like this: <BODY BGCOLOR=0000FF, LINK=FF0000 VLINK=00FF00 TEXT=FFFFFF> as shown in Figures A8-1a and A8-1b.

Figure A8-1a
Color Attributes using Words
B - Enter BGCOLOR and a value
C - Enter LINK and a value
D - Enter VLINK and a value
E - Enter TEXT and a value

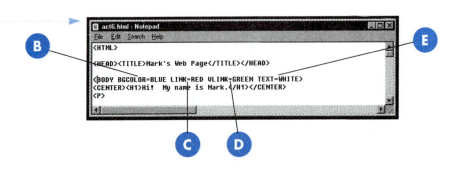

Figure A8-1b
Color Attributes using Hexidecimal Numbering
B - Enter BGCOLOR and a value
C - Enter LINK and a value
D - Enter VLINK and a value
E - Enter TEXT and a value

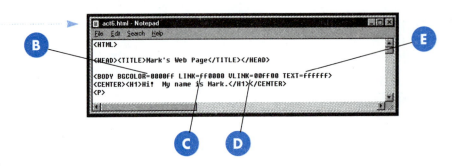

Step 4: Save the changes to your file. Name your new file **act8.html** or **act8.htm**.

Step 5: Switch to your browser and view how the changes will look on the Web. Did all of your colors display properly? Do you like the color choices? Try some of these other colors: white, black, red, yellow, blue, green, orange, purple. Some will work, some won't. The fun of HTML is experimenting to see what works.

Debriefing

Changing the background and link colors can add interest to your Web pages. Try different color combinations and see the effects of changing attributes and adding color values. Try creating the best color combination possible, then create the worst combination ever. Then, try different color values. For example, try other color hexadecimal numbers, like 007ABE. (ABE is Mark Web's nickname.) Experiment, experiment, experiment!

Extension: Open your Famous Quotes Web page (**act7.html** or **act7.htm**) and change all of its color attributes. Add to your Web page. Create some hypertext links on your Famous Quotes Web page that link to other pages of information about these three famous people.

Graphics and Gimmicks

Graphics can enhance Web pages in many ways. **Graphics**, a computer term for pictures, can make the difference between an exciting and a dull Web page.

There are several ways to put graphics into your Web pages. First of all, you can simply reference the location of a graphic on the Web and insert it in your document. When the browser is reading your HTML tags, it will notice one that says, "Go and get this picture or graphic at this remote location and display it here." For example:

```
<IMG SRC ="http://www.thomson.com/swpco/IMAGES/abe.gif">
```

This is an easy way to use graphics off the Web, BUT WATCH OUT! Capturing graphics this way puts an unnecessary load or burden on the Web server that hosts the graphics. Why? Because your browser must run to the Web every time it wants to display a picture. To use graphics this way is considered rude.

A better way to use graphics is to copy them to your computer's hard drive HTML-?? folder. If your Web page and picture are in the same folder, then the command is much smaller. For example:

```
<IMG SRC="abe.gif">
```

This method not only saves you a lot of typing, it is also much more Net friendly. With the graphics files on your local computer, you don't have to bother the Net with unnecessary requests for your pictures or graphics.

You can also create your own pictures in a drawing program. You can then convert the file in a graphics program like Adobe PhotoShop or CorelDraw into a Web graphics format. You must save your pictures in one of the special Web formats, usually .gif or .jpg. Sometimes .jpg is spelled out .jpeg. Each of these file types will work on the Web.

You can even take digital pictures with a digital camera, save them as .gif or .jpg file types and put those digital pictures in your Web page. Just remember to save all of your files in your HTML-?? folder.

If you have a picture you like, you can also use a scanner to make a digital copy of the image. Save your scanned pictures as .gif or .jpg files and you can use them just like pictures you take from the Web.

Objectives:

- Copy **levy.gif** to your HTML-?? folder.
- Create an inline image of **levy.gif**.
- Use attributes and values to reduce the size of **levy.gif**.
- View your final creation.

Activity 9 · Putting Images in Your Page

Step 1: Start your Web browser and your text editor.

Step 2: Open your Web page text document called **act8.htm** or **act8.html**. Save a new copy of this file as **act9.htm** or **act9.html**.

Step 3: Switch to your Web browser.

Step 4: Go to the *HTML Activities Web Page* at

http://www.thomson.com/swpco/internet/markweb.html

Step 5: Click on the Activity 9: Putting Images in your Page link. You should see a dragon. (Actually he is a sea monster called a Leviathan.) His name is Levy. To borrow a copy of **levy.gif**:

5A: If you are on a Windows computer, click the right mouse key on Levy's nose. If you are on a Macintosh, click and hold your mouse key on Levy's nose.

5B: Different browsers use different terms for the same Save Image command. You may see any of the following:

- **Save Picture As** (Figure A9-1a)
- **Save Image As** (Figure A9-1b)
- **Download Image to Disk**

Figure A9-1a
Save Picture As in the Internet Explorer for Windows

Figure A9-1b
Save Image As in Netscape for Windows

Step 6: Save your **levy.gif** file on the same disk and folder (HTML-??) as your **act9.htm** or **act9.html** file.

Step 7: To place the image **levy.gif** into your Web page:

7A: Return to your text editor and position your cursor (blinking line) just before the close body tag </BODY>.

7B: Enter the image search tag <IMG SRC="levy.gif"> as shown in Figure A9-2.

Figure A9-2
IMG SRC Tag with the levy.gif Value

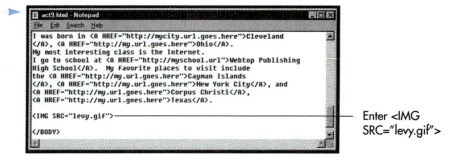

Enter <IMG SRC="levy.gif">

Step 8: Save your work.

Step 9: Switch to your browser and view how the **levy.gif** picture will look on the Web. Were you able to add a graphic? How big is your graphic? (See Figure A9-3.) Too big? To make your graphic smaller and to position the picture on the page, use the attributes described in the Table of Tags for Activity 9.

Figure A9-3
Levy is a bit too big! It's time to cut him down to size.

Table of Tags for Activity 9		
Image Search	<IMG SRC="">	Searches an image on your computer or on the Web.
Align Attribute	ALIGN=	Aligns pictures with the text.
Height Attribute	HEIGHT=	Determines the height of a graphic.
Width Attribute	WIDTH=	Determines the width of a graphic.

9A: Return to your text editor. Use the ALIGN=, HEIGHT=, and WIDTH= attributes to change the position and size of your graphic as written here: <IMG SRC="levy.gif" ALIGN=RIGHT HEIGHT=100 WIDTH=100>

9B: Switch to your browser and view how the changes will look on the Web. Were you able to change the size of the graphic? How big is your graphic now?

Step 10: Save and close your Web page and your Web browser.

Debriefing

You can add lots of graphics to your Web pages. Remember to use graphics that are only **public domain** pictures. This means that you have permission to use the graphics you borrow. Try finding a picture of Martin Luther King, Mother Teresa of Calcutta, or Winston Churchill on the Web. Copy these graphics to your HTML-?? folder or directory. Add these pictures to your Famous Quotes Web page.

Extensions
1. Experiment with the width, height, and alignment of your pictures. Alignment can be a bit tricky. When you use the align attribute, you are aligning a picture to its closest related text. You can use ALIGN=TOP, ALIGN=MIDDLE, ALIGN=BOTTOM values. Try each one. What does each do? How do these values change the effect?

2. Create a hyperlink! Use the following string of tags and attributes to turn Levy into a hyperlink that goes to my (Mark Web) Web page:

<AHREF="http://www.thomson.com/swpco/internet/markweb.html"><IMG SRC="levy.gif"></A>

When you view the change in your browser, you will notice a slight border (usually blue) around the picture. If you click on the picture, you will link to my Web page!

ebbing Around

In Activity 3 you learned about the Webtop Publishing Process or IPTCP. Use this method to create a new Web page of your own using all the skills you have learned during Activities 1 through 9.

1. **Investigate** your topic.

2. **Plan** your Web page.

3. **Take a look around** for new ideas.

4. **Create** your Webtop publication.

5. **Publish** on the Web.

O b j e c t i v e s :

- Create the coolest Web page ever created.
- Use a sample of every attribute and tag you have learned so far.
- Add graphics and images to your Web page.

▸ **Step 1: Investigate your topic**

Surf the Web in search of a personal top ten list of Web pages. Pick the ten pages you like the best. Collect the following information about each:

A. What is the URL for each of the top ten Web pages?

B. What is the title of the Web page?

> **Hint!** Look at the Title Bar on the top of your browser window.

C. Why do you like this page?

D. Why should someone else visit this Web page?

E. What are the file names for any .gif or .jpeg files that are okay to display on your Web page?

Write all of these details down in your official notebook.

▸ **Step 2: Plan your Web page**

Plan out how you want your page to look in a Web browser. Decide what tags you are going to use and where. Since this is a top ten list, you may wish to use an unordered list or an ordered list. The placement of graphics is always important. Where do you want to align them? Where do you want graphics to appear? Also, you may wish to write a paragraph or two about your selections.

Add paragraphs and descriptions, even quotes, to your page about your links. Let the reader of your page know where they are going and why you think it is a cool Web site.

Activity 10 Favorite Places to Go

Step 3: **Take a look around for ideas**

Return to the Web and your top ten links often and look for ideas. Remember to click the View Source command. You can also take any graphics from my Web page!

Step 4: **Create your publication**

Enter your starting tags and begin! Try to follow your plan. However, if you get a new idea, try it! Remember to save and test your Web page frequently. Use the following file name: **act10.htm**.

Step 5: **Publish on the Web**

Publish your Web page for the world to see! However, this step may not be easy for you if you don't have a local Webmaster. For more information on the process required to publish on the Web, refer to Appendix B.

Debriefing

By the end of this activity you have mastered the basics of HTML tagging. It is time to move on to more sophisticated tools that can make it much easier for you to create better and better Web pages.

Don't forget to view the source of your favorite Web documents to see how the special effects on the Web page were created.

Also, never forget where your text editor is. You may still need it. Sometimes you will create a Web page and something just looks wrong. Often, the best way to fix a bad page is to look at the tags in your trusty text editor, SimpleText or Notepad. More sophisticated tools often hide what is going on inside the tags of the page. Keep that text editor handy!

The Tools of HTML Professionals

In this sector, you are going to leave the amateurs behind and begin to explore the professional world of Webtop publishing. Before you can graduate to the professional ranks, you may have to leave the comfortable world of Notepad and SimpleText behind and adopt a powerful HTML Editor.

HTML Editors include a spectrum of software programs that help Web authors make Web pages. You will have a chance to learn about many of these Webtop publishing software tools in Activity 11. Frankly, some HTML Editors are much better than others. After you test-drive a few editors, you will be able to make a good choice as to what tool best suits your style and needs.

If you don't have an HTML Editor, don't be too concerned. You will still be able to complete all of the following activities with Notepad or SimpleText. However, at some point in time, you will want to make use of the features a good HTML Editor can provide.

Sector

2

In Chapter **4** *The Right Tool for the Job* will help you make an intelligent choice when picking an HTML Editor.

In Chapter **5** *Using your HTML Editor* will show you how to transfer what you already know about HTML to your HTML Editor.

The Right Tool for the Job

Mark Web will introduce you to the world of HTML Editors. Then he will take you on a tour of the Web in search of the right HTML Editor for you. After his report, you will be able to investigate for yourself the strengths and weaknesses of many of the popular HTML Editors in hyperspace.

This chapter will explore the questions:

- What is an HTML Editor?
- What are freeware, shareware, and professional HTML Editors?
- What makes a good HTML Editor good?

A good HTML Editor can make Web page creation much easier and more fun. An HTML Editor may work for some Webtop authors and not work for you. You decide which HTML Editor will best suit your needs.

O b j e c t i v e s :

- Analyze various HTML Editors.
- Examine how HTML Editors are similar to and different from word processors.
- Investigate improvements to HTML including Microsoft and Netscape extensions.
- Evaluate HTML Editors.
- Visit HTML Web sites on the WWW.

Casting Notepad and SimpleText Aside! (details at 11:00)

"Millions and millions of Web pages currently on the WWW were created with simple text editors like Notepad for Windows, or SimpleText for Macintosh. There are many professional Webtop publishers who refuse to use anything else. These "true-grit" professionals have memorized countless tags, attributes, and codes. One top-notch Webtop author exclaimed, 'Why should I use an HTML Editor? That would make HTML too easy. I will stay with Notepad.' "

"Despite this comment, even top-flight professional Webtop authors, designers, and publishers need to investigate HTML Editors for one big reason — HTML Editors can help them complete their Webtop publications more quickly. After all, in the Webtop publishing business, time is money."

What is an HTML Editor?

An HTML Editor is a special text editor or word processor that is customized for Web page creation.

While there are many powerful HTML Editors, no single HTML Editor does it all. Webtop professionals often use a variety of tools to help them. A Webtop publisher may:

1. Start a Webtop publication with one HTML Editor, then

2. Switch to Notepad or SimpleText to clean up a few things, then

3. Switch to another HTML Editor to add the final graphics, inline images, and multimedia effects.

To be helpful, an HTML Editor must be:

- Practical
- Easy to use
- Powerful

Practical

An HTML Editor must fit your situation. For example, if you only create a few Web pages a week, then an expensive professional-level HTML Editor that costs several hundred dollars would not be practical.

Likewise, if you are constantly creating Web pages as part of your school work or as part of your job, then creating your Web pages in Notepad or SimpleText would simply take too much time.

To be practical, a Webtop author needs to consider which HTML tool best fits their situation, and download or buy an editor to fit their needs.

Easy to Use

An HTML Editor should make your life as a Webtop publisher easier, not harder. Many Webtop professionals have purchased a new HTML Editor only to find that it is easier to enter tags in Notepad or SimpleText. They can't find the features they need, or the logic of the program is so confusing as to defy understanding.

This is why you will want to try an HTML Editor before you buy it. Most editors can be test-driven before you have to pay to use the product. You can save a lot of time and frustration by taking advantage of these free trial offers. There are many easy-to-use HTML Editors on the market. If an HTML Editor isn't easy to use, then throw it away and search for a new one.

Powerful

HTML Editors should have:

1. Lots of bells and whistles,

2. Lots of extra horsepower,

3. Lots of new ways to get things done!

HTML Editors must be powerful. Quality HTML Editors should do more than enter basic HTML tags. They should include all the latest extensions to HTML provided by Microsoft and Netscape. As HTML grows and changes, your HTML Editor should improve right along with it. Therefore, the company that created your HTML Editor should allow you to download upgrades and improvements to their product from their Web page on the WWW.

Similarities and Differences Between Word Processors and HTML Editors

Examine a typical word processor, like Word, WordPerfect, or WordPro. Word processors automatically insert codes (like tags) into the text as you type a letter or your English report. In some word processors, you can select a command called "Reveal Codes." This command allows you to see the little tags or codes inside your word processing document. This is very similar to the **View Source** or **View Document Source** commands in most Web browsers.

"Hmmm...if you are thinking to yourself, 'Word processing codes must work a lot like HTML tags,' well, you are correct."

The principles behind word processing codes and HTML tags are similar, with a couple of very important differences:

1. Word processing codes define pages to be printed by a printer, while HTML tags describe Web pages to be displayed on the World Wide Web.

2. Word processors use their own method of marking up text. Therefore, every different kind of word processor creates its own unique file type, often indicated by a special file name extension. For example, Word uses the .doc file name extension. WordPerfect uses the .wpd file extension. HTML is the standard way Web authors use to present their pages on the Web. HTML documents carry the .htm or .html extension.

It didn't take a rocket scientist to figure out that word processors and HTML Editors can work together. All the major word processors now have HTML Editors built into their word processing software. These HTML tools make it easy to convert your word processing documents into HTML documents.

The two major word processors, Word and WordPerfect, both have HTML capabilities. For example, Microsoft created the Internet Assistant for Word, Corel created the Internet Publisher for WordPerfect.

Isn't life great? Now you can do word processing and HTML at the same time. Well, perhaps it isn't all that great. Not just yet, anyway.

HTML Editors are not as developed as word processors. Word processors have been around a decade longer than HTML Editors. They have more experience doing their job. Also, word processors typically only have to worry about a computer and a printer. HTML Editors must worry about all the different computer platforms and browsers that reside on the Web. In short, HTML Editors must conform to HTML 2.0 and HTML 3.0 standards, or the WWW falls apart. So don't expect your HTML Editor to be as easy to use or as powerful as your favorite word processing program.

Four Kinds of HTML Editors

Activity 11 takes you onto the WWW to investigate HTML Editors of all kinds. There are four main categories of HTML Editors:

- HTML Editors you can have for free (often called "freeware").
- HTML Editors that may cost you a little (often called "shareware").
- HTML Editors that will cost you a lot more (including professional tools you might buy in a store.)
- Professional HTML tools that come "bundled" with other powerful software programs (like the HTML Editors found in word processing software packages).

Freeware HTML Editors

HTML Editors can be found all over the Web for free. These editors are called **freeware**. They consist of software programs that someone has written (perhaps as a project for a college degree) and made available free of charge over the WWW. If you find one of these editors, you can download it and use it at no cost.

Shareware HTML Editors

Shareware is the second type of HTML editing software available to you on the Web. The concept of shareware is simple. Normally, you can try a program for a limited period of time absolutely free. If you like the software, you can buy it. If you don't like it, you can simply delete it from your computer.

Shareware HTML Editors are extremely popular and a wide variety of good ones appear on the Web.

Professional HTML Editors

There are a growing number of HTML Editors that are considered professional tools. These can be expensive depending on which one you buy. They offer features that the shareware and free versions often overlook. For example, many of the professional HTML Editors offer customer support and free upgrades for a period of time after purchase.

Prices can vary. For example, Adobe's PageMill will cost you a few centavos. But, PageMill is significant because it was the first dedicated WYSIWYG HTML Editor. More and more HTML Editors are WYSIWYG, allowing you to see what the finished Web pages look like before you view them on the Web.

Microsoft offers a professional-level HTML Editor called FrontPage. FrontPage has lots of extra power and back-end support. The phrase "back-end support" refers to tools built into the Web server software. FrontPage goes beyond the conventional HTML tool and offers links to many other Microsoft Web server software tools. It allows you to organize a Web site and manage it.

Bundled Professional HTML Editors

A bundle means that two or more pieces of software are included together. The major software companies bundle HTML Editors into their word processing programs. The best known of these bundled HTML Editors are:

- The Internet Assistant for Microsoft Word
- The Internet Publisher for Corel's WordPerfect

If you have Word or WordPerfect, you can usually download and install a companion publisher or assistant that converts your word processor into a powerful HTML Editor for free.

Taking a slightly different approach, Netscape Communications Corporation bundles an HTML Editor with its popular Netscape Navigator. This bundle allows you to create, view, test, and save Web pages in the same software program.

Netscape normally makes versions of its Navigator available free to educational institutions. Companies and individuals are asked to pay for the software. Depending on your status, you may have to pay for the version of Netscape that includes an HTML Editor.

Evaluating HTML Editors

There are several things you need to consider when you evaluate an HTML Editor:

- How much does it cost?
- Does it conform to HTML standards and include Microsoft and Netscape extensions? For example, can this editor do forms, tables, inline images, sound, video, Java, Shockwave, JavaScript, and CGI? (See FAQs on Java, JavaScript, Shockwave and CGI.)
- How easy is it to test or view Web pages and then edit those pages?
- Will it convert word processing documents into Web pages easily?
- Is the HTML Editor a WYSIWYG or an enhanced text editor?

FAQs

What is Java?

ava is a programming language used on the World Wide Web. Java allows a programmer to create application programs that can run any kind of computer over the Internet. Java is rapidly becoming a standard tool for programmers who want to share programs over the Web.

FAQs

What is Shockwave?

hockwave allows graphics to move on your Web page documents. Shockwave can add excitement to your Web pages by manipulating graphics and grabbing the attention of your audience. One of the first Shockwave graphics to move was a tornado.

Cost

As you learned earlier, there are freeware, shareware, professional, and bundled HTML Editors. How much you spend on an editor is entirely up to you. However, before you spend a lot of money, think about what you are trying to accomplish. If you are planning to be a professional Webtop author and publisher, and you have a few extra dollars laying around your house or apartment, buying a top-of-the-line HTML Editor may be to your advantage.

HTML changes all of the time. New extensions are always being added. If you purchase an HTML Editor today, chances are you will be buying additional upgrades tomorrow. Make sure that any editor you buy allows you to upgrade free of charge for a certain period of time after the initial purchase.

HTML Standards and Extensions

HTML is governed by a set of standards that tells the Web what features and tags are approved and acceptable. This rather lengthy process of approval helps insure that the Web is able to support Webtop publishing on the superhighway.

However, companies like Netscape and Microsoft live and die financially by being better and faster than their competition. They can't afford to sit around waiting for an international committee to set the new HTML standards. To be competitive, both Microsoft and Netscape have added what are called **extensions** to HTML. Extensions include many new features that are not supported (yet) by the international Web standards committee. Extensions give extra power to Microsoft's and Netscape's WWW tools. Your HTML Editor should be able to take advantage of these extensions.

Another class of tools is being developed for the Web which go beyond HTML. Java and Shockwave are adding moving objects and application programs to the WWW, making it a more enhanced multimedia environment. Be sure that any Web editing tool you use supports these new enhancements to the WWW.

Testing

Your HTML Editor must allow you a simple way to test your Web pages. To be an expert Webtop author and publisher, you will need to know how your Web page will look to another person on the Web half a world away. Your HTML Editor must have a convenient way to slip into a browser and view the page. Testing should be easy and hassle free.

Conversion of Word Processing Files

Converting existing word processing documents isn't really all that difficult. If worse comes to worse, all you need to do is copy your word processing document and paste it into Notepad or SimpleText and enter the required tags.

However, the Internet Assistant for Word and the Internet Publisher for WordPerfect make it even easier to make those conversions. Since most documents in the world were created with one of these two word processors, it makes sense to investigate using them to convert your regular documents into HTML Web pages.

Is Your Editor a WYSIWYG?

Companies like Adobe, Microsoft, Netscape, Corel, and others are trying to help Web authors and publishers get a better idea of how their work will look once it is posted on the WWW. To do this, they use Graphical User Interfaces or GUI software. GUIs (pronounced gooey's) are examples of WYSIWYG software.

You should consider selecting a GUI-WYSIWYG HTML Editor. A GUI-WYSIWYG HTML Editor goes beyond the entering of simple <TAGS> in ASCII text. GUI-WYSIWYG allows the movement and manipulation of objects, like pictures and words, around your Web page. Using a GUI-WYSIWYG Editor is like using a powerful word processor or a desktop publishing program to create Web pages. Text editors are limited. WYSIWYG will allow you to see what your Web pages will look like on the Web as you create them. This is very important if you are using pictures and graphics, or have many complicated pages to work with.

The Limits of WYSIWYG

GUI and WYSIWYG are very popular. It is nice to be able to see exactly what you are going to get before you post it on the Web. However, there are a few Web-imposed limits on WYSIWYG in cyberspace. "What You See Is *Sort of* What You Get" in cyberspace. WYSISWYG, pronounced "wizzy-swig," is a more accurate description for several reasons:

1. No one can predict which of the many Web browsers web users will be using.

2. Many people haven't updated their browsers recently. Older versions of widely used browsers usually don't have many of the required features needed to handle sophisticated and high-tech Web pages.

3. No one can predict if a person viewing a Web document is on a Macintosh, a Windows machine, a UNIX, or a SUN computer station.

4. Since people can change the size of their browser windows, no one can predict how big the window will be once the images come into a browser.

5. The end user can also change their screen preferences in most browsers.

6. Browser users can change colors, font sizes, and other variables that will change the look of Web pages when they load them into their computers. This may change the look of the Web pages you create.

FAQs
What is CGI?

GI is computer talk for Common Gateway Interface. CGI takes advantage of forms on the WWW. For example, when you fill out a form on the Web, you will pass information from the Web to a database somewhere in cyberspace. CGI provides a script which allows the HTML Web page to communicate the information you enter to the database.

FAQs
What is JavaScript?

avaScript is not the Java programming language discussed earlier, but a way to use programmer-like commands inside the HTML text itself. JavaScript works more like an extension to HTML than a programming language. JavaScript is fun and easy to learn. It is compact and efficient. JavaScript works like little Java applet programs. There are some great applications you can use that were created in JavaScript.

FAQs

Why are there so many different options on the Web?

ost of the computer, software, and preference options existed on the Internet before the Web was born. The miracle of the Web is that it continues to work despite all of these differences. With so many options, computer platforms, Web browsers, and individual preferences, it is a wonder that anyone can communicate at all!

Essentially, true WYSIWYG on the Web is impossible. *Therefore, when you create a Web page, view it from several computers, like Macintosh and Windows, and view it in several Internet browsers.* See how it looks on someone else's computer.

For example, when creating a Web page for a key client, one Web author found that graphics are often displayed differently by the Internet Explorer browser as opposed to Netscape. Also, when visiting a college in another region of the country, this same Webtop publisher discovered that a Web page that looked great on a home computer became distorted and unreadable when combined with certain color preferences used by the college. *You have to account for computer and browser differences if your Web pages are going to be read and enjoyed by the widest possible audience.*

Using a WYSIWYG HTML Editor is a great way to go, but there is one additional problem. Sometimes WYSIWYG hides what is really being added to the Web page on the HTML <TAG> and text level. Web authors who depend too much on WYSIWYG editors can create HTML editing nightmares. If they never look at the HTML tags underneath the Web page, they may not ever know how the Web page really works. And, for some problems at least, the only way to solve a tricky HTML problem is to look at the tags and remove or move the problem tags. This is why many professional Webtop publishers continue to work directly with the HTML tags, using Notepad or SimpleText as their main software tool.

Debriefing

The truth is, most of the Web pages currently on the WWW were created with simple text editors like SimpleText and Notepad. But, to be fast, a professional must be armed with the latest and greatest HTML Editors. HTML Editors can save a lot of time, and for professionals, that means money!

In Activity 11, you will go out onto the WWW and search for HTML Editors using search engines. Keep track of what you find while you are searching the Web. This information will allow you to keep up on any improvements made to HTML and to your Webtop publishing software tools.

he Search is On!

The HTML world is changing all of the time. To participate, you must learn how to stay informed on all the changes that are constantly occurring.

HTML Editors and information about those editors can be found all over the Web. In this Webtop publishing activity, you will take a quick trip to the *HTML Activities Web Page* and see what is listed there; then you are off on a hyperspace tour of the Web, looking for the latest and greatest HTML software tools.

Using a search engine, you can find many examples of shareware and freeware HTML Editors. More importantly, you can find lots of info on HTML itself and on the various HTML extensions and improvements. In addition, you can find new products that are making the Web an even more exciting place to visit. In this activity, you will collect 10 URLs that point to HTML literacy.

The search is on!

O b j e c t i v e s :

- Start your Web browser.
- Visit the *HTML Activities Web Page.*
- Locate some prominent HTML commercial editors' Web pages.
- Use a search engine to find shareware and freeware HTML Editors.
- Collect URLs from 10 different HTML Editor sites and add them to your Web page.
- Save your work as **act11.html** or **act11.htm**.

 Step 1:   Start your Web browser.

Step 2:   Find the *HTML Activities Web Page* at:

> **http://www.thomson.com/swpco/internet/markweb.html**

Step 3:

Click on the *Activity 11: The Tools of the Webtop Publisher* or the *Search Engines* links. There you will see a list of search engines to choose from. Select any one of the search engines on the list and start searching.

Step 4: When your search engine appears, enter five of the words or phrases below, one at a time, in the search engine's search window. Submit the search and see what information appears for each topic.

- HTML
- HTML Editors
- Word Internet Assistant
- WordPerfect Internet Publisher
- PageMill
- Netscape Gold
- HTML Guides
- Learning HTML
- HTML Extensions
- HTML 3.0 Standards
- Java
- Visual J++
- Shockwave
- CGI
- JavaScript

Step 5: Find ten Web pages that have useful information about HTML and HTML Editors.

Hint! Focus in on the specific HTML Editor you will be using in Chapter 5.

FAQs

What is a Search Engine?

A search engine is a software tool that allows you to search for Web pages on the Internet. Search engines are easy to use. Simply enter a word or several words into the window provided in the engine and click the search button. The search engine then runs out and finds all sorts of Web pages that contain the information you are searching for. When searching, spelling counts. Make sure you spell any search words correctly.

	Web Page Title	Web Page URL
1		
2		
3		
4		
5		
6		
7		
8		
9		
10		

Follow the Webtop Publishing Process steps to create a Web page of information about HTML, your specific HTML Editor, and other HTML extensions and improvements.

HTML Webtop Report!

You are about to become a Webtop reporter. Webtop professionals often create their own Web pages to track specific areas of their industry. By going to their Web pages, they can quickly find out what's new and important for them to consider.

Earlier in this activity, you created a list of ten URLs that point to HTML sites on the Web that provide information on HTML, HTML Editors, and other features about HTML.

However, don't just make a simple list. Give some background and information related to each hypertext link you include on your page.

► **Step 6:** **Investigate your topic**

You have already searched and found your URLs and titles for this Webtop activity. Visit each site in your list of ten sites and make notes about each editor or HTML topic. Here are some sample questions you can use to guide your report:

A.   What is the name of the HTML Editor?

B.   What is the name of the company that makes it?

C.   How much does it cost?

D.   What are its reported strengths?

E.   What are its reported weaknesses?

F.   Would this be an editor to recommend to a professional, to an amateur, or to a novice Web page creator?

► **Step 7:** **Plan your Web page**

Plan how you want your page to look in a Web browser. Since you are including text and links together, decide if hypertext links in lists are appropriate or if hypertext links inside paragraphs would communicate better. Limit the length of your paragraphs.

► **Step 8:** **Take a look around for ideas**

Get a few ideas from the Web pages you have visited. Include graphics that are appropriate in your on-line report. Look at how others use tags to create new effects.

Hint! Visit the *HTML Activities Web Page* and click the Activity 11 link. There you will find some great Web page examples to look at.

► **Step 9:** **Create your Webtop publication**

Open Notepad, SimpleText, or your HTML Editor and enter your tags. Save and name your new file **act11.html** or **act11.htm**.

► **Step 10:** **Publish on the Web**

Get with your Webmaster and post your Web page. Visit Appendix B if you need more details on how this is typically done. If you don't have access to a Web server, then keep a local copy of it instead and use it when you need it.

Debriefing

You now have a Web page dedicated to keeping up on the latest innovations in the Webtop publishing industry. Even if you can't place this Web page on the Web, you can still use it from your computer's hard drive to access your most important HTML sites. It you use this page from time to time, you will be better informed and always stay state of the art!

Extension: Pick another topic of personal interest and create a Web page on it. What other top-ten lists can you think of creating? Can you create a series of top-ten Webtop pages that explore individual topics? Here are some ideas:

Top 10 History Sites

Top 10 Math Sites

Top 10 Literature Sites

Top 10 Art Sites

Top 10 Game Sites

Top 10 Music Sites

Top 10 Sports Sites

Top 10 School Sites

FAQs

What is a Webmaster?

A Webmaster is a person who manages Web pages on Web computers called servers. Web servers communicate directly with the Web. Without a Web server, you won't be able to have your page seen by the outside world of the Web. A Webmaster keeps web servers working and helps post, or place, Web pages on the server so they work properly and can be accessed by interested visitors to the Web.

Using Your HTML Editor

This chapter focuses on using *Internet Assistant for Word* as your HTML Editor. It allows you to do so many things better and faster. For example, Internet Assistant for Word:

- Lets you easily convert existing word processing documents into HTML documents.
- Provides tool and menu bars that give you easy click and double-click access to many of the key HTML tools and commands.
- Is a WYSIWYG editor, so you can get a good idea of how a Web page is going to look as you are creating it.
- Has a great scheme for creating hypertext links and bookmarks quickly and in an organized way.
- Allows you to "see the tags" with a click and a double-click.

Internet Assistant for Word makes creating Web pages easier. The Internet Assistant passes the three tests of a good HTML Editor listed in the previous chapter. It is:

- Practical
- Easy to use
- Powerful

O b j e c t i v e s :

- Get an overview of Internet Assistant for Word.
- Manipulate the basic HTML tags with Internet Assistant for Word.
- Implement various graphic and WYSIWYG features.
- Create bookmarks and hypertext links with Internet Assistant for Word.

Internet Assistant for Word's Remarkable Speed

"I have found the Internet Assistant for Word to be a powerful ally in the creation of Webtop publications. The thing I like most about the Internet Assistant is that it is fast. I can change a word processing document to an HTML document in a matter of seconds. I can also add links and bookmarks faster with Internet Assitant. Zip-zip-zureei, and I am finished."

"If I need to see the HTML tags, I can, without having to leave Word!" (See Figure 5-1.)

"The Internet Assistant also makes the creation of backgrounds and the inclusion of graphics into a Webtop publication extremely easy. In short, I love it!"

Do You Have a Copy of Internet Assistant for Word Already?

Start by checking to see if you already have a copy of Internet Assistant for Word installed in your copy of Word. This is done by opening Word and clicking on the File menu. Look for clues like *Open URL* or *Browse the Web* as shown in Figure 5-2.

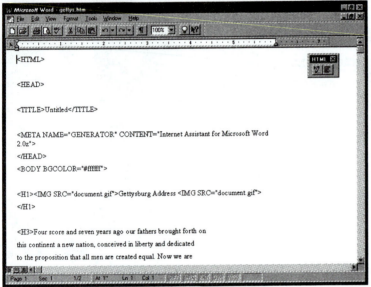

Figure 5-1
The Starting Tags in Internet Assistant for Word

Internet Assistant for Word changes your copy of Word into an Internet browser. If you are connected properly to the WWW, you can use Word to surf the Web.

If you have these options under the File menu, try the command **Browse Web**. When you make that selection, you will come to an easy-to-follow tutorial about creating HTML documents in Internet Assistant. (See Figure 5-3.) Spend a few minutes reading and trying the various features and suggestions.

Figure 5-2
Open URL and Browse the Web options in Word

How Do I Download or Update Internet Assistant for Word?

But what if you don't have Internet Assistant for Word? Word users can download free updates of Internet Assistant for Word from Microsoft. If you click on the Chapter 5: Using Your HTML Editor link on the *HTML Activities Web Page*, you will see a link called Download Internet Assistant for Word. From there you can link to Microsoft and get a recent copy of Internet Assistant for Word.

The URL to the *HTML Activities Web Page* is:

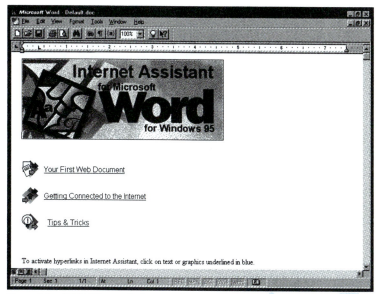

Figure 5-3
Browsing with Internet Assistant for Word

> http://www.thomson.com/swpco/internet/markweb.html

Even if you already have a copy of Internet Assistant for Word, you should visit this site every now and then to see if updates and improvements have been made. The URL for Microsoft is:

> http://www.microsoft.com/msword/

Downloading is easy if you follow these few steps:
1. Find the Microsoft Word Web page as listed above.
2. Find the link to the Internet Assistant for Word on the Word Web page.
3. Click on the Download link and read the information provided.
4. When you feel ready, click on the Download link.
5. A copy of the Internet Assistant (IA) for Word will be downloaded to your computer.
6. Double click on the Internet Assistant for Word installation program icon or run the **Add Programs** utility on your computer and select the setup program you downloaded from Microsoft.
7. Follow the instructions in the Setup Wizard. That's it. Open Word and see if your update appears.

Debriefing

In this chapter, you learned a little bit about Internet Assistant for Word and how to download and install updates of this valuable addition to Word. In the activities that follow, you will quickly learn to use this powerful HTML Editor.

sing HTML in Olympic Fashion

 Assuming that you have the latest version of Internet Assistant for Word installed correctly on your computer, it's time to start it up and create a few WYSIWYG Web pages.

This activity demonstrates how to accomplish some of the familiar HTML commands you learned in Sector 1 quickly and easily with Internet Assistant for Word.

The theme for Activities 12-14 is the Olympics. ("It must be noted that in the last Olympics, I, Mark Web, Investigative Reporter for The WebTop Times, won the gold for the best HTML reporting at the Olympic games.")

Start this project by searching for ten Olympic links. Then, using Internet Assistant for Word, start a report Web page about the Olympics.

O b j e c t i v e s :

- Search ten great Olympic sites on the WWW.
- Create a report using Internet Assistant for Word.
- Use the following WYSIWYG commands for:
  - Starting Tags
  - Formatting Tags
  - Break Tags
  - List Tags

Step 1: Start your Web browser.

 Hint! If everything is set up correctly, you can use Word as a Web browser. Click **Open URL** from the File menu, enter a URL and fly to your site. However, most Word users still use their Web browser to surf. Word is slower in cyberspace than a regular browser.

Step 2: Find the *HTML Activities Web Page* at:

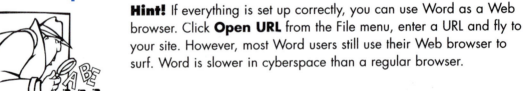
http://www.thomson.com/swpco/internet/markweb.html

Step 3: Click on the Search Engines link. Select any one of the search engines on the list. **Hint!** If you need help, review Activity 11.

Step 4: When your search engine appears, enter the following Olympic words and see what information appears on each topic.

- Olympics
- Olympics Ancient Greece
- Olympics Summer
- Olympics Winter
- Olympics Atlanta
- Olympics Nagano Japan
- Olympics Salt Lake City
- Olympics Sydney Australia

Step 5: Find ten Web pages that have information about the Olympics and record the title and URL for each selection here.

	Web Page Title	Web Page URL
1		
2		
3		
4		
5		
6		
7		
8		
9		
10		

Step 6: Open Word.

Step 7: Select **New** from the **File** menu.

Step 8: To open a Word HTML document:

8A: Select **Html.dot** from the **New** document dialog box as shown in Figure A12-1.

8B: Click **OK**.

Hint! Make sure you have selected the General tab. If you don't see **Html.dot**, then Internet Assistant may not be installed properly.

Figure A12-1
Select **Html.dot** from the **New** Document Dialog Box
A - Select **Html.dot**
B - Click OK

General Tab

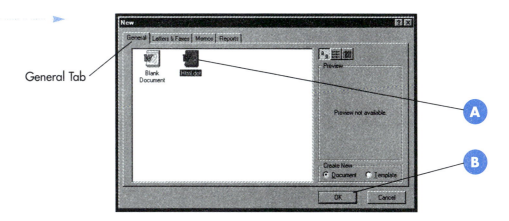

Note: Notice how the button bars in Word change when you are working in the HTML Internet Assistant.

Step 9: To enter a title for the Title Bar of your Web page:

9A: Click the **File** pull-down menu.

9B: Select **HTML Document Info . . .**

9C: Enter *Olympic Research Paper* in the Title field as shown in Figure A12-2.

9D: Click **OK**.

Figure A12-2:
Enter the Title
C - Enter Olympic
Research Paper

Step 10: To enter a level 1 heading <H1> called *Olympic Links*:

10A: Type *Olympic Links* at the top of your Web page.

10B: Select *Olympic Links* by clicking and dragging with your mouse.

10C: Click on the Heading 1 button or select **Heading 1, H1** from the **Style** drop-down menu on the **Formatting** toolbar.

10D: Click on the **Center** button on the Formatting toolbar.

FAQs

What and where are the Standard and Formatting toolbars?

Word has several toolbars that help you with your HTML work. First, there's the Standard toolbar (see Figure 12-3). The Standard toolbar lets you save, copy, paste, and many of the other things you are familiar with when you are word processing. The Formatting toolbar gives you several HTML specific commands. Make sure this toolbar is visible as you work (as marked in Figure 12-3). To make these toolbars appear, select **Toolbars** from the **View** pull-down menu. When the **Toolbars** dialog box appears, click a check mark next to **Standard** and **Formatting**.

Figure A12-3
Create a Heading 1 and Center the Text
A - Key Olympic Links
B - Select Olympic Links
C - Click on Heading 1
D - Click Center

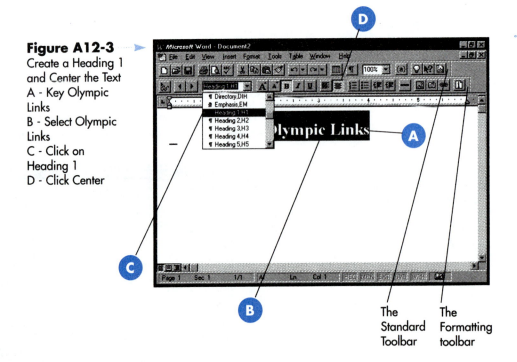

The Standard Toolbar

The Formatting toolbar

Step 11: To enter your list of Olympic titles:

11A: Press Enter/Return to create two spaces between your H1 heading *Olympic Links* and the start of your list.

11B: Enter your first Olympic title. Press Enter after each line as in Figure A12-4.

Figure A12-4
Enter Your Olympic List
A - Press Enter twice
B - Press Enter Once

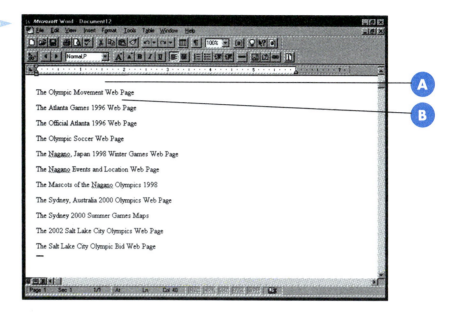

Step 12: To create a bulleted, or unordered, list:

12A: Select your ten titles as shown in Figure A12-5.

12B: Click on the Unordered List or Bulleted List button.

Note: That's it! That is all there is to it. Slick, huh! No more entering <LI> tags!

Figure A12-5
Create a Bulleted or Unordered List
A - Select your 10 titles
B - Click the Bulleted List button

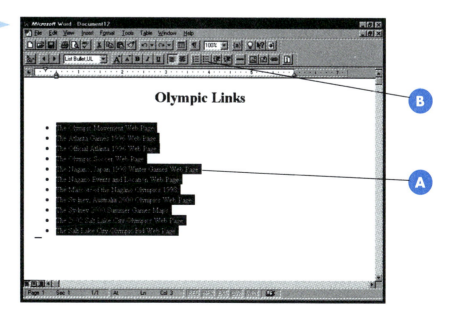

Step 13: Enter a horizontal line between your H1 title, Olympic Links, and your list.

13A: Position your cursor or mouse pointer between the list and the title.

13B: Click on the **Horizontal Rule** button from the Formatting toolbar as shown in Figure A12-6.

13C: Position your cursor or mouse pointer at the end of your list and add a space by pressing Enter/Return.

Note: If another bullet appears, simply backspace to delete it.

13D: Click on the **Horizontal Rule** button.

Figure A12-6
Adding a Horizontal Line
A - Position cursor
B - Click the Horizontal Rule button
C - Position cursor and add a space
D - Create Horizontal Rule
15 - Click HTML Source to see the tags

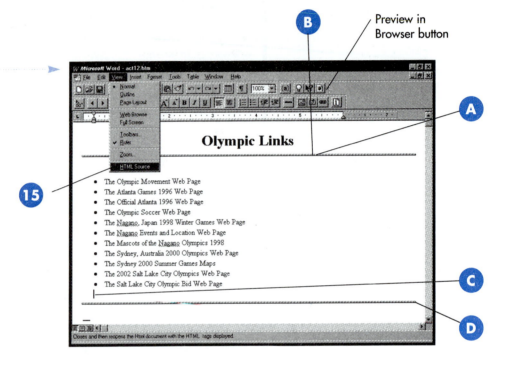

Troubleshooting

Now that you are using a WYSIWYG HTML Editor like Word's Internet Assistant, it is important to troubleshoot your work. To do this effectively, you must view the tags in their natural HTML state.

Although you can't see them, Internet Assistant for Word has just entered a bunch of HTML tags for you, like, <HTML>, <HEAD>, <TITLE>, <CENTER>, <H1>, <P>, <HR>, and many more. The tags have been entered behind the scenes! Do you want to take a look?

It is important to save your work before you start looking at the tags. Click **Save As** from the File menu. When the **Save As** dialog box appears, click until you find your HTML-?? folder or subdirectory and save your file as **act12.htm**.

Note: Word for Windows 95 or higher will accept long file names, so you can use the .html extension if you want to, but it is probably easier to stick with the shorter and traditional .htm extension.

Step 14: Save your work by selecting **Save** from the **File** menu.

Step 15: Click **HTML Source** from the **View** menu as shown in Figure A12-6. The HTML tags will soon appear as in Figure A12-7. View all of the tags you didn't have to enter. (Cool, huh!)

Figure A12-7
Viewing the Tags
16 - Auto Format Button
18 - Return to Edit Mode
Button

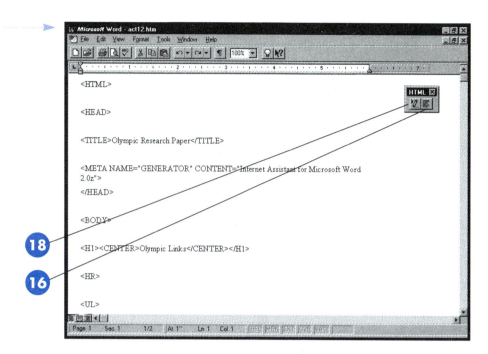

Step 16: To auto format your document, click the **Auto Format HTML** button or select **Auto Format HTML** command from the **Format** menu.

Note: The **Auto Format HTML** is a great feature. Your HTML links change colors so you can see them easily!

Step 17: Scroll down and look at your tags. Do you see any tags you don't remember from Sector 1? Do you see any errors? If you do, make the corrections you need to make.

Step 18: Switch back from HTML Source Mode to the WYSIWYG mode by clicking the **Return to Edit Mode** button or pick the **Return to Edit Mode** command from the **View** menu.

Note: If you have made changes, Word asks you to save before you return to edit mode.

Step 19: Open your new Web page in your Web browser and see how it looks. You can get to your Web browser quickly by clicking the **Preview in Browser** button as shown in Figure A12-6.

Hint! If everything is installed correctly, your browser should appear with your Web page in it. If not, don't despair. Simply open your browser and preview it the old-fashioned way like you did in Sector 1.

Debriefing

You have learned the basics of using Internet Assistant for Word to create Web pages. You have seen Word's tremendous versatility in being able to switch back and forth between HTML mode and WYSIWYG mode.

If you don't like the colors in your Web page, go back and change them. Make any corrections, additions, or deletions you have time for.

Extension:

Here is another important thing you can try — converting an existing Word document into an HTML document.

Step A: Open Word, then open an existing Word Document.

Step B: Select **Save As**. In the **Save As** dialog box, select HTML (.htm) from the **Save as type** window as displayed in Figure A12-8.

Step C: Click **Save**.

Figure A12-8
Converting a Word Document to an HTML Document
B - Select **.htm** from the **Save as type** window

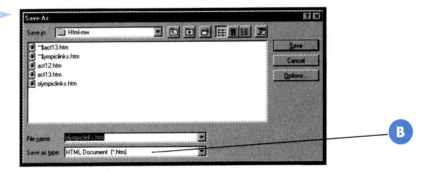

Presto! You have converted your document into a simple HTML document. As you return to your document, you will notice the Word toolbars change to the HTML Internet Assistant toolbars.

You can also copy information from a regular Word document and paste the information into another HTML document. This is important.

For example, if you have already completed a report on the Olympics, you can copy part of your report and move it to your HTML report.

ight Up Your Olympic Coverage

"Now that you have started your Olympic Web page, it is time to light up your coverage with a little background creativity. You will find that manipulating colors and creating links in Internet Assistant is faster than an Olympic bobsled from Jamaica."

O b j e c t i v e s :

- Open an existing HTML document in Word.
- Create hypertext links in your Olympic Web page.
- Change the color values for:
  - The background
  - The text
  - The links
  - The visited links
- Add a graphic to your Olympic Web page.

Step 1:   Start Word.

Step 2:   Open your Olympic Links document **act12.htm**.

Step 3:   Save a copy of your document as **act13.htm**.

Step 4:   To create links from the items in your Olympic Links:

4A: Find your list of URLs you compiled in Activity 12, Step 5.

4B: Select the first item in your list with your mouse. (See Figure A13-1.)

4C: Click on the **Hyperlink** button as marked in Figure A13-1, or click **Hyperlink** from the **Insert** pull-down menu.

4D: Enter the URL that applies to the first item in your list in the **File or URL** window in the **Hyperlink** dialog box as indicated in Figure A13-1.

4E: Click **OK**.

Figure A13-1
Creating Hypertext Links
in Word
B - Select the first name in
the list
C - Click the Hyperlink
button
D - Enter your URL
E - Click OK

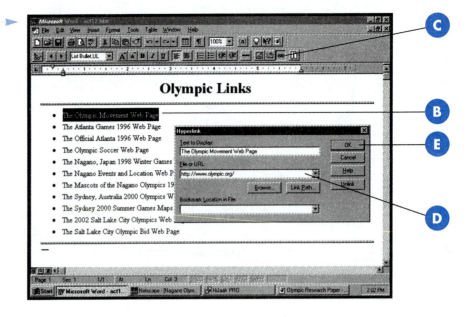

Figure A13-1
Creating Hypertext Links in Word

4F: Repeat Steps 4B through 4E and enter in URLs for every title on the list.

> **Step 5:** Save and preview your Web page. Test each link on the Web to make sure it works. Return to Internet Assistant for Word to make any necessary corrections.

Troubleshooting

If you make an error entering your URL in your hypertext links:

A: Click once on your bad link to highlight or select it.

B: Select the **Hyperlink** link button (or pick **Hyperlink** from the **Insert** menu).

C: In the **Hyperlink** dialog box (see Figure A13-1), correct the URL in the **File or URL** window. You can also correct the text or title of the **Text to Display** window.

Follow the steps to change the background and link colors in Word.

> **Step 6:** To change the background and link colors in Internet Assistant for Word:

6A: Click the **Format** pull-down menu.

6B: Click the **Background and Links** command as shown in Figure A13-2.

Figure A13-2
The Background and Links
Command
A - Click Format
B - Click Background and
Links . . .

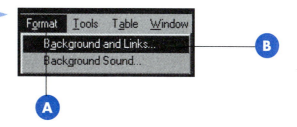

6C: Click the **Background Color** down arrow to display the list of color choices. Scroll down the list and select the color yellow as shown in Figure A13-3. (Admittedly, not the best of background colors, but you can change it to something you like better a little later.)

6D: Change the **Body Text** color to blue. **Note**: This is the same as the <TEXT> attribute.

6E: Change the **Hyperlink to pages not yet viewed** color to magenta. **Note:** This is the same as the <LINK> attribute.

6F: Change the **Hyperlink to pages already viewed** to dark blue using the drop down menu as shown in Figure A13-3. **Note:** This is the same as the <VLINK> attribute.

6G: Click **OK** after making your color selections.

Figure A13-3
Changing the Background
and Links Colors
C - Click Background
Color
D - Change Body Text
E - Change Hyperlink
F - Change Viewed Link
G - Click OK

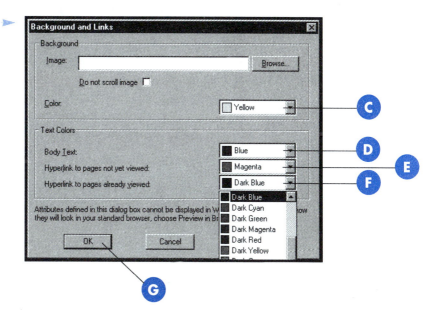

Step 7: Save your changes and view your color changes in your Web browser. How do they look? That yellow background may be a bit too much, don't you think? Return to Internet Assistant for Word and make your own color choices.

Step 8: To add a graphic or a picture to your WYSIWYG Web page in Internet Assistant:

8A: Visit my Web page and select the <u>Activity 13: Faster Links, Colors, and Graphics</u> link.

> **http://www.thomson.com/swpco/internet/markweb.html**

8B: Download the file **rings.gif** (the picture marked in Figure A13-6) . Save it to your HTML-?? folder.

> **Note:** If you need help with this process, revisit *Activity 9: Putting Images in Your Page.*

> **Hint!** Some versions of Internet Assistant for Word seem to prefer .gif files to .jpg files. For this example, use the .gif version.

8C: Return to Internet Assistant for Word and open your **act13.htm** Web page.

8D: Position your cursor or mouse pointer just above the first Horizontal Rule or line as shown in Figure A13-4.

8E: Click the **Center** button to move your cursor to the middle of the page. Now you are ready to go get your picture.

Figure A13-4
Adding a Graphic to Your WYSIWYG Web Page
D - Position Your Cursor
E - Click Center Button
F - Click Picture Button

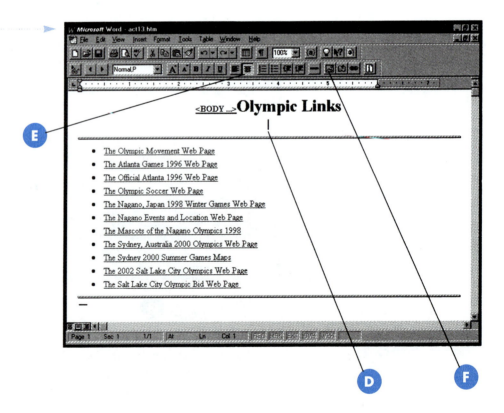

8F: Click on the **Picture** button as shown in Figure A13-4. (You can also select the **Picture** command from the **Insert** pull-down menu.)

8G: When the **Picture** dialog box appears, click the **Browse** button as marked in Figure A13-5. The **Insert Picture** dialog box will appear as in Figure A13-6.

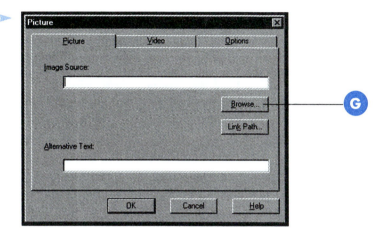

8H: Locate your HTML-?? folder in the **Insert Picture** dialog box as shown in Figure A13-6.

Hint! Use the buttons marked as **Hint!** to navigate your folders in Windows 95 until you find your HTML-?? folder.

8I: Select your file, **rings.gif**.

8J: Press **OK**. You will be sent back to the Picture dialog box.

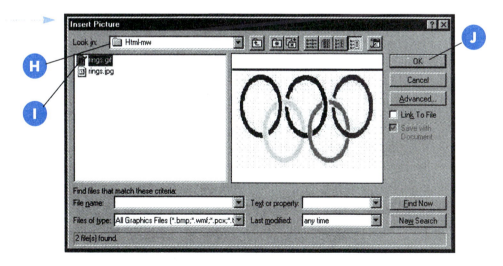

8K: Enter the words Olympic Rings in the **Alternative Text** window as marked in Figure A13-7.

Figure A13-7
Entering Alternative Text
in the Picture Dialog Box
L - Click OK

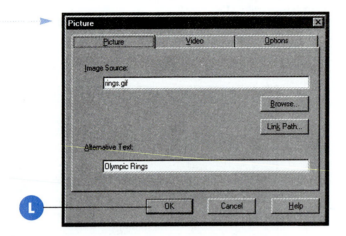

Note: The alternative text is displayed if someone tries to view this page with their **Images** turned off in their browser. This is the HTML <ALT=> Attribute. This is very helpful for people who have a slow Internet connection or if the page doesn't display the graphic or picture properly.

8L: Press **OK** to close the **Picture** dialog box as shown in Figure A13-7.

8M: Your graphic should appear in the center of your page as displayed in Figure A13-8.

Figure A13-8
Graphic Appears in Web
Page

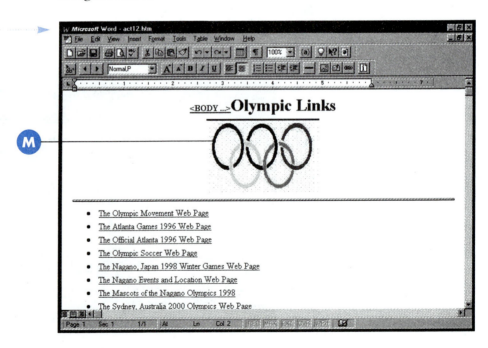

Hint! If there is an error, simply press the Undo command in Word and start over.

8N: Save your work and view your changes in your Web browser. (Remember to use the **Preview** button!)

Debriefing

You now know how to do all of the skills you learned in Sector 1 using the WYSIWYG HTML Editor known as Internet Assistant for Word.

The Internet Assistant won't totally free you from working with <TAGS>. Remember to use the **View, HTML Source** command to view the tags easily from inside Word. You can also view the <TAGS> in Notepad if you like.

Extension: Go back and change the color values in your **act13.htm** Web page. Find colors that match and that work together well. Make sure the links are easy to see. Good luck!

Go for the HTML Gold

Internet Assistant for Word has many, many features. To learn them all will take you weeks. How can you find out about these new features?

The best way to learn how to use Internet Assistant for Word is to try something new and see how it goes. In other words, click on the button and see what happens. Save your work before you start experimenting so you don't lose any of your changes.

When you get totally stuck, go to the on-line help. Click the Help pull-down menu and try several of the options.

Figure A14-1
The Help Pull-down Menu

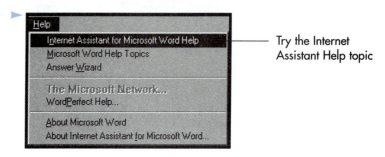

Try the Internet Assistant Help topic

For example, why does Word save with the .htm extension instead of the .html extension? Well, actually, Word can work with both file extensions. Click the **Index** tab as marked in Figure A14-2 and enter .htm vs. .html extension and see what appears.

Figure A14-2
The Index of Help Topics
Select .htm vs. .html
extension

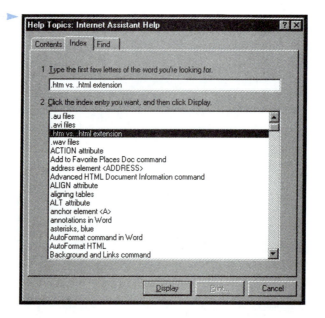

The answer you are given is shown in Figure A14-3.

Figure A14-3
The .htm vs. .html Help
Topic Answer

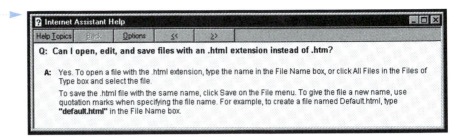

Try some other topics, like:

- BGCOLOR Attribute
- HTML, Defined
- Hypertext
- Internet Assistant, Commands

Use the IPTCP process to add to your Olympic Web page using Word's new features. Use your Help options and learn new skills and techniques.

Step 1:   **Investigate your topic**

You have already searched and found your URLs and titles about the Olympics. Before you start, open **act13.htm** and save it as **act14.htm**.

Visit each site in your list of ten sites and make notes about each Web page. Copy and paste important information to your word processor where you can change and manipulate it. Make sure you give credit for any quotes.

Here are some questions that can guide your investigation:

A. What is this Web page about?

B. What is the name of the company or organization that maintains the Web page?

C. When quoting this page, who should get the credit?

D. What kind of information or content resides on this site?

E. What are the highlights or strengths of this Web site?

F. What are the weaknesses of this Web page or Web site?

G. Would you recommend this site to others? Why or why not?

Step 2:   **Plan your Web page**

Plan how you can improve your existing Olympic Web page. Does it need paragraphs explaining the various topics? Does it need more graphics? Where should these pictures appear? Since you are including text and links together, think how links inside paragraphs would work and how to create those in the best way. Limit the length of your paragraphs. Don't make them too long.

Step 3:   **Take a look around for ideas**

Borrow a few ideas from the Web pages you have visited. Use the **View, Display Source** or **View, Display Document Source** options to view the <TAGS> that other people have used.

Step 4: **Create your Webtop publication**

Make your additions and creations to **act14.htm**.

Step 5: **Publish on the Web**

Post your Web page presentation. If you don't have access to a Web server, then keep a local copy of it instead and display it when you need to. See Appendix B for more information about posting Web pages.

Debriefing

As you go for the gold, try and learn as much about HTML as you can by looking at other Web pages. View the document source and see what new tags you can utilize in your Webtop publications.

At this point you are prepared with the basics on HTML and you know how to use a sophisticated HTML Editor. Use all the tools at your disposal to make your pages outstanding.

Extension: Pick a new topic and prepare a Web page from scratch using your HTML editing tools and knowledge. Here are some possible topics:

- The American Civil War
- The European Economic Community
- Problems in the Middle East
- Technology in Japan
- The best educational Web pages from your state or province

Use the IPTCP process. Start by using your search engine to **Investigate** the topic. Then, **Plan** your page. **Take a look around** for new ideas as you search, then **Create** your page. When you are all done, **Post** your page.

Webtop Publishing on the Superhighway

Very few people had heard of the World Wide Web before 1993. In 1994, a Web browser called Mosaic became popular on the Internet. Mosaic software displayed Web pages with graphics and pictures. (What a concept!) This software tool generated a worldwide interest in the WWW. Mosaic was a freeware graphical browser that became the predecessor to both Microsoft's Internet Explorer and Netscape's Navigator.

In 1995, business discovered the value of the Web. Millions of new Web enthusiasts caught their first glimpse of the Web through Prodigy, America Online, and CompuServe. By this time, Netscape Communications Corporation had created a faster browser. When Netscape went public, by allowing people to buy stock in their company, they shocked the computer world by making its founders multimillionaires in a matter of hours. Later that year, Microsoft released Windows 95, which provided a Web browser called the Internet Explorer. They also offered Windows 95 customers access to the newly created Microsoft Network or MSN. The WWW had become a major computing and telecommunications phenomenon in record time.

The Web has continued to grow and change, perhaps more rapidly than any other communications medium in world history. The popularity of the Web was fueled by Webtop authors and publishers, the creative people who made all of the wonderful Webtop pages and presentations. Creative people like you.

In Chapter **6** *It's About Art, Technology, and RESPECT* will examine Web art in three categories — words, multimedia, and layout. The complexities and ethical responsibilities of Internet technologies are viewed from the eyes of a Webmaster.

Activities 15 through 23 present all sorts of new challenges and interesting things to do in HTML. Stay tuned for the following:

Activity 15: Pictures as Web Art (Getting the .GIF of the Page)
Activity 16: Creating an Organized Layout (Linking to Anchors)
Activity 17: Window Frames (Three Pages in One)
Activity 18: Informational Pages (Setting Your Table on the Net)
Activity 19: Form Design (What Do You Need to Know?)
Activity 20: Check Boxes (Click Yes, Click No, Click I Don't Know)
Activity 21: Animate Your Web Page (Cartoons of the Web)
Activity 22: The Java Ride (We're Not in HTML Anymore, Toto!)
Activity 23: So, How Was That? (Tags, Tags, Always Tags)

Sector 3

Chapter 6

It's About Art, Technology, and RESPECT

"I was showing some of my favorite Webtop presentations to some people one day when a listener stopped me and asked, "This Web thing, it's really about art then, isn't it?"

"As a full-time reporter for The WebTop Times, I had to agree. Communicating and expressing yourself by words, pictures, and sounds can become an art form."

"So far, you have been creating simple Web pages, the kind of pages anyone can create. Now you will begin to see what is required to take your documents to the next level."

O b j e c t i v e s :

- Learn what makes up a compelling Web site.
- Review how words can become Web art.
- Review how pictures can add to your Web art.
- Review how interesting layout can add to your Web art creations.
- Discuss how technology and art combine on the Web.
- Discuss the many responsibilities of a Webmaster.

The Essential Elements of Great, Compelling Web Sites

You can easily identify a great Webtop publication from a simple Web page by the following characteristics:

- Well-written text
- Exciting graphics and multimedia effects, including animation, sound, and video
- An interesting, easy-to-follow layout on the screen

These elements combine to share ideas and information with Web page viewers. (See Figure 6-1.)

Webtop publishers know they have only about three seconds to grab someone's attention and get them interested in the Web page presentation. They also know that Web surfers come back to a Web site that's interesting, informative, and compelling.

A compelling Web site is any site that keeps people coming back again and again. A compelling Web site can be created by:

- A company (.com)
- An organization (.org)
- A school (.edu)
- A government agency (.gov)
- The military (.mil)
- An individual like you

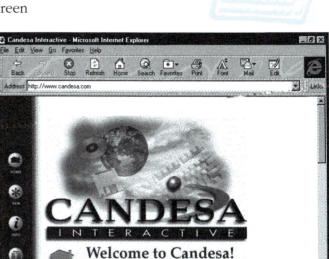

Figure 6-1
Candesa Interactive Specializes in Creating Compelling On-line Imagery

Making the graphics, special effects, words, and layout work together to create an exciting site is the challenge of every Webtop publisher.

A great Web site presents information in an interactive way. The term "interactive" means that the person who visits the Web site:

- Becomes involved
- Makes decisions
- Is presented with choices
- Participates in the Webtop presentation in a meaningful way

This is one reason why Webtop publishing is different and exciting. Desktop publishing normally works only with a printed page of paper. In the electronic world of the Web, you can be much more creative in developing Webtop presentations. You can create links, add video and sound, and involve the user by having them select from a variety of choices. Each time a visitor to a Web site makes a choice, it changes the way the Webtop presentation works.

Every visitor can have a different experience at the site. Web surfers should come away from a site feeling that the Webtop presentation was created specifically to meet their needs. One of the best examples is www.disney.com. It is not only a site for children; people of all ages can

go to the site and see something that interests them. You can find everything from video releases to investor information for those who own Disney stock. Think of it this way. With a quality Webtop presentation:

- Everyone has a slightly different experience
- Each visitor makes individual choices
- Every surfer generates a personal perspective of the material being presented
- Web surfers enjoy the Web site so much that they recommend the URL to others

If the graphics are appropriate, the words communicate clearly, and the Web pages link well together, you have a professional Webtop publication or presentation.

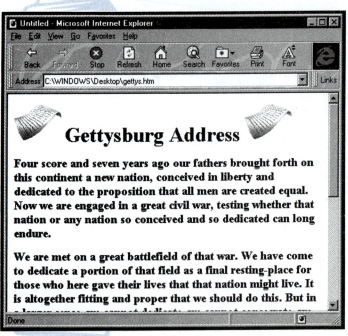

Figure 6-2:
Lincoln's Gettysburg Address on the WWW

Words as Web Art

Well-written text was nearly absent in the early days of the Internet. You could find many technical reports, conversations, commentaries, and technical specifications. However, very few of the early Internet and Web pages were clear, concise, or communicated well to a broad audience of Web page readers.

Today on the Web, all that has changed. Businesses started the trend toward well-written Web pages. The last thing a business wants is to have a Web page full of spelling and grammar errors, or worse, post a Web page that is so technical that no one but the Web technicians can understand it.

There is room for nearly any style of writing on the WWW. You can find poetry, literature, even your favorite on-line magazine. You can also find some of the great speeches, like:

- Abraham Lincoln's *Gettysburg Address* (Figure 6-2)
- Martin Luther King's *I have a dream* speech
- Quotes from *Mother Teresa of Calcutta*
- Excerpts from Churchill's wartime radio addresses

Words can become an art form on the Web. The key for a Webtop publisher is to take the written words and present them in a way that is appealing to the reader. (You will read more on this in the *Layout as Web Art* section that follows.)

Webtop authors must write well. They must anticipate who their audience is and calculate how visitors will respond to the words on the Web pages. They must also consider how links to other Web pages can enhance the Webtop presentation.

There are many different writing styles on the Web. Some sites reflect technical writing, other sites follow a journalistic tradition, other sites are reserved for creative writing.

Pictures as Web Art

When it comes to the WWW, a picture is worth a thousand words. In just a few seconds, Web surfers will decide if a site has value for them. Remember this: **On the Web, the Web surfers or viewers are always in control.** They can click their mouse and move to another Web page in a matter of seconds. If a Web page doesn't attract their attention, the visitor will click the mouse and be off to a new Web page.

Think of it this way. How many words can you read in three seconds? Not many. This is where pictures can help. A picture is worth a thousand words *if* it can hold a Web surfer's attention and get them interested in learning more.

Great graphics help attract attention and help explain the contents of a Web page to the viewer. Excellent graphics give Web surfers confidence in the quality of the site and compel them to return often.

The multimedia effects you see on the Web are only the beginning. Words like Java, Shockwave, and CGI are becoming as common to your vocabulary as apple pie and the World Wide Web. The multimedia capabilities of the Web will help redefine the way we share information, the way businesses operate, and the way we learn.

Naturally, you can't get away from words entirely. You can overdo graphics and depend on them too much. The two elements (words and graphics) must blend expertly to create the most powerful impact on Web site visitors. And this is where layout comes in.

Layout as Web Art

Layout is the art of making a page look great while communicating its message clearly. Logical layouts give a Web page organization and order. Layout can also make the Webtop publication easy to follow. Some of the options you will learn about in this chapter can help organize the layout of your Web site, including:

- Tables
- Frames
- Forms
- Internal Links

In the early days of the Web, a nice layout was a difficult thing to create. HTML had not been invented yet, and there were no WYSIWYG tools to help you layout a nice Web page. Even early HTML was primitive by today's standards. Originally, HTML was developed to describe a text document to browsers on different computer platforms. Since the WWW is a worldwide system, when you posted a Web page you couldn't be sure if the page was being displayed by a Macintosh computer, a DOS machine, a Windows computer, or a UNIX workstation.

In addition, early Web browsers were not very powerful! Some early browsers, like Lynx, didn't even display graphics. Many early competitive Web browsers displayed the same information in different ways. What a mess!

Ideally, to do true layout, you should know exactly how the page will look when it is displayed at the other end of the cyber line in a graphical browser. As you learned in Chapter 4, HTML cannot always provide a true WYSIWYG environment. Rather, the Web is more of a WYSISWYG — What You See Is *Sort of* What You Get. You must try and account for:

- Different browsers
- Old and new versions of popular browsers
- Different size windows
- The personal preferences of Web surfers

The activities that follow will help you implement HTML tags that will give you more control over what the browser displays, and will allow you to create more interactive designs and layouts. In the discussion that follows, you will learn how the technology of the Web can affect your layouts.

"It's About Technology, Too . . ."

The Web is a merger, a blend of two elements — art and technology. As Web technology changes, the ability of Webtop publishers to express themselves and to create polished web impressions improves and improves. This constant enhancement is caused by improvements in the technologies of the Web. They include:

- Better Web browsers
- Better understanding of how the Web works
- HTML standards
- Popular extensions

Building Better Web Browsers

Mosaic was the first popular graphical or GUI Web browser. Graphical simply means that it could display graphics or pictures. It was created at the National Center for Supercomputing Applications at the University of Illinois. Several key people from the Mosaic programming team went to work for Netscape Communications Corporation and created a faster browser called Netscape. Netscape set new standards for browser excellence in the mid-1990's.

Mosaic wasn't dead yet, however. The browser was improved by several companies and became known as the Enhanced Mosaic browser. Eventually, Microsoft released a greatly enhanced version called the Internet Explorer in 1995.

These new browsers have more power and abilities than Lynx or Mosaic. Netscape and Microsoft keep adding capabilities to their browsers called extensions. Extensions allow many new kinds of displays over the World Wide Web.

A Better Understanding of How the Web Technologies Work

Many early Web page writers didn't understand how the Web worked — how all the hardware and software of the WWW work together. As a result, many pages didn't work. In those days, rather tacky "Under Construction" graphics dotted the Web as Webtop publishers tried to fix the many problems in their Webtop presentations. In the projects that follow, you will learn more about how the Web functions. This understanding will help you construct better-looking Webtop publications.

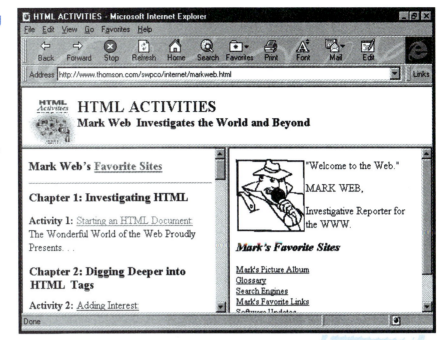

Figure 6-3
HTML 3.0 Allows Frames like These to be Constructed. Frames Help Organize Several Pages Together in one Browser Screen.

HTML Standards

An international group meets and sets standards for the World Wide Web. These standards are known by numbers HTML 1.0, HTML 2.0, HTML 3.0 and so on. Once standards are set, the software companies will include the new features so that their browsers conform to the new international standards.

HTML 3.0 is a new set of HTML standards that allow HTML to do more. These new standards allow Web publishers to add tables, forms, and a variety of other features to Web pages (see Figure 6-3).

Popular Extensions

During the years that it took for HTML 3.0 standards to be defined, Microsoft and Netscape began defining standards of their own. These standards are called extensions to HTML. Certain extensions became popular. As they did, they were included in other browsers.

Independent development created some problems since some extensions could only be read by Netscape users and others could only be read by Microsoft Internet Explorer users. Older browsers that did not have these new extensions were out of luck. The impact of competition often means that some Web pages can only be viewed optimally with one browser or another. Also, some important features may simply be unavailable until the next version of the browser program comes out.

Nevertheless, these extensions helped improve the layout and design capabilities of Web pages. People using browsers that supported these new extensions could view better Web pages.

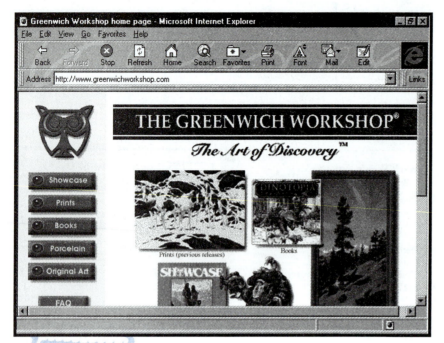

Figure 6-4

The Greenwich Workshop Encourages the Art of Discovery

This page clearly presents its interactive options to the viewer.

Working With The Limitations

Look at this sample page (see Figure 6-4). Does it gain your interest? Do you want to click on one of the pictures or buttons? Does it make you curious? Do you instantly understand the options presented — Showcase, Prints, Books, Porcelain, Original Art, and FAQ? Which button would you click on first?

Remember, most Web surfers decide in seconds if the site can help them or not. Given that fact, a few things you need to remember about Web page layout include:

1. Attract your viewers' attention quickly.

2. Make the key points easy to find.

3. Make your page easy to navigate.

4. Make your content easy to read.

5. Your graphics should support your text.

6. Your text should support your graphics.

The process of placing your Web pages on a Web server is called "posting." In order to "post" a page, you must have access to a Web server. Normally, you will contact a person called a Webmaster who will help you post your pages. (See FAQs: What is a Webmaster?) You will have to ask around to find out who your Webmaster is. They are considered gurus. You shouldn't have much trouble locating yours. (For more information about posting Web pages, see Appendix B.)

It's About Responsibility, Too . . .

Webmasters and Webtop publishers carry a great deal of responsibility. Since Web pages can be viewed by anyone, anywhere in the world, Webmasters and Webtop publishers must be careful that the information and images they post are appropriate and worth reading. The essence of what is considered good form and practice on the Web can be spelled out by the phrase "RESPECT the Web."

R = The Responsibility test

E = The Everybody test

S = The Simplicity test

P = The Purpose test

E = The Ethical Use test

C = The Correctness test

T = The Totally Cool test

Does Your Page Meet the Seven Tests of Web RESPECT?

R = The Responsibility Test

As a Webmaster or Webtop publisher, you assume certain responsibilities. No single person, group, company, or government agency owns or controls the content of the World Wide Web. It is up to Webmasters and Web publishers to ensure that the Web is a people–friendly place for information, entertainment, and learning.

The main Webtop publisher responsibility is to ensure that a Web site adds to the value of the Web as a communication resource.

A Webmaster must not allow unprofessional and unethical pages to appear on a Web site. This can become a difficult task, but by using the six "tests" represented by the rest of the letters in the word RESPECT, the job can become easier.

E = The Everybody Test

If you are in doubt about a Web page, ask yourself this question, "Will *everybody* who has access to the Web page appreciate it or enjoy it?" If you feel that some people may be offended by the page in a personal way, you need to consider changing the page to make it more acceptable to your audience.

The Everybody Test is easy to administer. If you have any questions about how your Web page may be received by people, ask them! Ask visitors what they think of the content and imagery of your page; ask them to look at it. Let them express their opinions. Then, show them you value their opinions and comments and make the positive changes they suggest.

FAQs

Once again, what is a Webmaster?

A Webmaster is a skilled technical person who operates and manages a Web server. Most Webmasters started out creating Web pages, just like the ones you have created. Later, they "got into" the technology and learned how the "back-end" or Web server software works. These highly trained and skilled people manage complex and interesting Web sites for companies, Internet service providers, schools, and government agencies. Without Webmasters, the Web would cease to function. Webmasters can serve as both the local Webmaster (technical consultant) and as a Webtop publisher (creative Web page consultant). Your Webmaster is your number one support person for your Webtop publishing efforts.

You can easily receive comments from Web page viewers by putting a "mail to" command into each Web page. For example:

```
<P>
If you would like to comment about this Web page, e-mail
<A HREF="mailto:MarkWeb@swpco.com">Mark Web, Investigative
Reporter for The WebTop Times</a>.
<P>
</BODY>
</HTML>
```

You will soon learn that different people will have many different opinions. You may not be able to please all of the people all of the time. Nevertheless, you should try to make your Web site a place that everyone can enjoy.

S = The Simplicity Test

The Simplicity Test has several levels.

- First, is the Web site easy to navigate? Can visitors to the site get around to the information they need quickly and easily? If it is hard to find information, your visitors will not stay around long and may never come back to your site again.
- Second, is the Web site easy to manage? The KISSS test can be applied to Web site organization and management. KISSS often stands for "Keep It Simple, Simpler, Simplest!"

The Web and Internet technologies are hard enough to figure out without adding unnecessary complexities. For example, the shorter and simpler the URL, the better:

The URL:

http://www.thomson.com/swpco/internet/markweb.html

is much better than the URL:

http://www.thomson.com/swpco/FILES/INTERNET/ htmlpages/books/wq56AB1:8001/~markweb.html

Some Webmasters employ unnecessary capitalization, add extra subdirectories, and complicate the site in a number of ways. Web technologies are complicated enough without adding to the difficulty. "Keep it simple, simpler, simplest!"

P = The Purpose Test

Every Web page should have a purpose, that is, it should make a point of some kind. Your purpose may be to sell a product or to talk about your favorite things. It may be to comment on the latest crisis in the Middle East. There are many ways to get your point across — with words, graphics, pictures, sounds, and even video. Whatever your purpose, make sure your page gets the main points across to the reader or viewer of your page.

The Purpose Test is easy to administer. First, write down the "point" or purpose of your Web page. What kind of message is it supposed to convey? What are you really trying to say or communicate? Then, have three friends visit your Web page. Have them write down what they think the purpose or point of the site is from their perspectives.

Compare your answer to your friends' responses. You will then know if the page communicates the purpose and key points you have in mind. If your page doesn't make the correct point or communicate your purpose, change the page. If the page makes no point at all, or serves no beneficial purpose, delete the Web page!

E = The Ethics Test

Unethical people can abuse the Web. Many people without a sense of community values place objectionable material such as pornography, hate group information, racially biased material, or prejudiced information on the Web. Some lie about products or services. Others try to cheat people by using the Web to promote nonexistent causes or scams.

What are the things you value? Write your values down in a list, and let this list guide you as you create your Web pages. By the same token, when you create your Web pages you need to ask yourself the following ethical questions. If the answer to any of these questions is no, then you need to change your Web page accordingly:

- Does my page conform to my values?
- Is the information on my page accurate and correct?
- Have I thought about my potential viewers and made an effort to eliminate objectionable material?
- Is my message honest?
- Is the information I am sharing beneficial?
- Is the information I am sharing legal for me to share with others?
- Do I give proper credit to others when I quote their work?

If the answer to any of the above questions is no, then you need to rethink and recreate your Web page.

C = The Correct Test

This test may seem obvious, but it is important none the less. Use the following list as a Correct Test for each Web page you create:

- Are all words spelled correctly?
- Does the writing conform to the rules of grammar?
- Do all the links work?
- Are all the contributors to the page recognized correctly for their work?
- Are all the pictures in the correct spot when the page loads?
- Is all the data presented on the Web page as correct and accurate as I can make it?

Can you answer YES to each of these questions? If so, you are on your way. If not, correct the errors before you post the page.

FAQs

What is a Flame?

Are there pages you have seen on the Web that offend you? If so, flame the Webtop publisher who created or maintains it. A flame is a time-honored Internet way to address concerns. A flame consists of a well-written comment, usually an e-mail, about a Web page you feel is offensive. Your e-mail should be delivered over the Net to the individuals involved. Express your opinion without being offensive. Specifically, list the elements of the Web site that bother you.

The best flames are controlled fires, not burning blazes of emotion and passion. In other words, don't rant and rave and stoop to vulgar language or rude comments when sending a flame. Simply write your feelings about the offensive material in the most sophisticated and polite way possible. These kinds of honest reactions will have much more effect on the Webmasters and Webtop publishers than the uncontrolled and unstructured comments often sent as flames.

T = The Totally Cool Test

The Web prides itself on being creative, innovative, exciting, and cool. One of the great values of the Web is that people can see what other people have invented on the Web. This creates a great deal of competition to see who can come up with a "better Web page."

The competitive atmosphere of the Web is tempered by the fact that Webtop publishers are normally happy to share their secrets with others. I, Mark Web, have never met a Webtop publisher or Webmaster who wasn't willing to answer a few questions or to give me a few suggestions. It is also hard for Webtop publishers to hide their work. Remember the **View Document Source** option on your browser? This enables you to view for yourself the tags that make another person's Web pages so cool.

While it is okay to get a few ideas, it is not ethical or legal to simply copy and paste or steal HTML code or Web graphics directly from a Web page without the express written permission from the Webtop publisher. Still, most are willing to help you improve your pages, so ask!

You can use any of the graphics or concepts found on my Mark Web Home Page. Permission granted! No need to ask. Help yourself.

The Mark Web Page is located at:

http://www.thomson.com/swpco/internet/markweb.html

You know when you have passed the Totally Cool Test when other people return to the Web page over and over and share your URL with their friends, colleagues, or business associates. You know you have *really* passed the cool test when someone actually bookmarks or adds your Web page to their favorite list!

Visit some of the totally cool pages I have marked on my Web page. Click the Chapter 6 Hypertext link and see the Web sites I find compelling:

http://www.disney.com/
http://www.lucasarts.com/
http://www.sony.com/
http://www.nbc.com/ (I love the peacock!)
http://www.yahooligans.com/

Debriefing

There are three elements that make up a good HTML Webtop presentation. They include well-written text, excellent graphics and multimedia effects, and an easy-to-follow layout. Each of these elements needs to combine intelligently to communicate in a concise, visual way, the message of the Web page presentation. In the next several activities, you will experience each of these elements of Webtop design.

The Web is about art, but it is about technology too. The blend of new technologies and creativity makes the Web an exciting, new canvas upon which you can express your ideas and demonstrate your imagination.

As a Webtop author, you need to practice lots of different approaches to Web site creation, try lots of new Webtop publishing tools and technologies, and find the best way to express yourself in this new medium. The best source of inspiration can be found on the Web itself. Some Web pages are wonderful, while many are a waste of time. Finding good WWW sites will help you gather ideas on how to best improve your HTML skills. Be sure to use the **View Source** or **View Document Source** commands to see the tags on new Web pages you discover.

As you grow in your Webtop creation skills, you will grow in your ability to persuade and influence others. This is called Webtop communication power. With this newfound power comes new responsibilities to RESPECT the Web and what it stands for — the communication of good ideas to everyone on planet Web.

Extension: Surf the Web and look for good examples of Web pages. Rank them into three categories:

1. Best text

2. Best graphics and multimedia effects

3. Best layout

Getting the .GIF of the page....

"If pictures are worth a thousand words, wait till you see how many words are on the Web."

"I have found the Internet to be full of .gif (Graphics Interchange Format) and .jpeg (Joint Photographic Expert Group) images. Extensions like .gif and .jpg are added to file names so they can be recognized and read by most Web browsers. Just like Windows displays .bmp graphic files, WordPerfect reads .wpg graphics, and Macintosh views .pict files, Web browsers can read and display either .gif or .jpg graphic files."

"It is exciting to create a Web page. When you do, you have created something that is yours. It is also very exciting to use graphics, especially when they are your own creations. Almost every page you visit will use graphics. When you create your own graphics and display them on your Web page, you will have a right to receive recognition for that graphic."

"In this activity, we're going to go to the Web and gather some .jpeg and .gif files. When you take objects from the Internet you need to make sure you give recognition to those who created them. Since I know of some great places to find non-copyrighted images, I will take you there and teach you how to download them. Ready to go grab some .gifs? Here we go."

Table of Tags for Activity 15

Background Tags	<BODY BACKGROUND=" ">	Create a background for your HTML document.
Image Search Tags	<IMG SRC =" ">	Place a desired graphic into your HTML document.

Objectives:
- Create folders to save images and files.
- Locate pages on the Internet to download images.
- Demonstrate the ability to download and reference images on the Web.

Create new folders in which to save Sector 3 projects and images:

Note: "Images" is another word for pictures, graphics, or icons.

Step 1: Create two new directories in which to save activities and graphics files:

1A: Locate the disk drive or floppy disk you will use to save your work and open it.

1B: Create a new folder called **projects**. Use all lowercase letters!

Hint! Folders are often called directories as in Figure A15-1. For Windows 95 or NT, select **File**, **New**, **Folder**. On a Macintosh, select **File**, **Create New Folder**. In Windows 3.1, select **File**, **Create Directory**. Remember to name the new folder or directory **projects**.

1C: Open the **projects** folder by double clicking on it. Create a new folder inside the projects folder named **graphics**. Keep the folder name in lowercase letters as in Figure A15-1.

Figure A15-1:
Create a New Folder
B - Create a projects folder
C - Create a graphics folder inside the projects folder

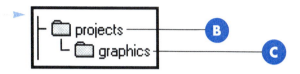

Step 2: Start your browser and locate .gif and .jpg files:

2A: Open your browser and find the *HTML Activities Web Page*. Scroll down and select the Activity 15 link.

http://www.thomson.com/swpco/internet/markweb.html

Hint! Use your Bookmark or Favorites list created in Activity 4 to help you locate the *HTML Activities Web Page* quickly.

2B: From the Activity 15 window, choose the first Hypertext link: Buttons, bars, and other icons. This Hypertext link takes you to a page with buttons, bars, and other icons you can download.

Note: This file takes a few minutes to load. It contains many bars and line breaks to use in a Web page. Be patient, but also be aware of the time it takes to load. Every image you insert in your page creates a longer download time to the Web user accessing your page. Too many graphics are worse than too few....just like too many words are oftentimes worse then just a few.

Step 3: After the Buttons, bars, and other icons Web page fully loads, complete the following:

3A: Read the text at the beginning of the page. It contains important information about downloading the images from this page.

FAQs

What is Plagiarism?

Plagiarism is the act of taking others' creations, whether in words, graphics, or software, and passing them on as your own. Copyrights are just as important on the Internet as they are on paper. You must be very careful about graphics, text, programs, and other objects you download from the Net. Whenever you are in doubt about using a graphic or a quote, create a reference to the Web page where it was retrieved and ask for permission to use the graphics and information you find.

3B: Scroll down the page and locate an image you would like to use in your Web page.

3C: Point your mouse at the image and click the right mouse button (Macintosh users point, click, and hold the single button).

3D: Choose **Save Picture As**, or **Save Image As**, or **Download Image to Disk** as you learned from Activity 9.

3E: Locate the folder or directory you created earlier named **graphics** and click **OK** or **SAVE** as directed in Figure A15-2.

Figure A15-2
Save As Dialog Box
E - Click OK

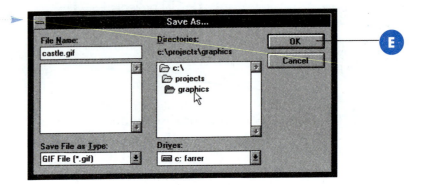

Hint! If you are using Windows 3.1, make sure the file name is only 8 characters long. You can change the name of the file to under eight characters or less; however, it is important that you do not change the extension of the file. The file extension is the three letters after the period in the name. Look at the example, **graphic.gif**. *Graphic* is the name of the file, *.gif* is the extension (or format) of the file and describes what type of file it is. You cannot change the extension. The file may become useless if you do. If you want to change the format of a graphic, you will need to use a graphic editor capable of reading and saving different types of graphics.

Step 4: Repeat the steps above to choose three different images on this page and save them in the **graphics** folder.

Step 5: Return to the *HTML Activities Web Page*. If you can't remember your way home, here are three ways to get there:

- If it is your Home page, click the **Home** button.
- Use your **History** or **Go** option and select it from the list.
- Press the **Back** button — it may take several clicks to return.

Step 6: To find and download additional graphics:

6A: Locate the Activity 15 hypertext link again and select it.

6B: Choose the link Graphics, Lines, & Backgrounds for your Home page.

6C: After the page loads, scroll down the screen and choose the link called Backgrounds.

6D: Wait for this page to load. (Again, it may take several minutes for all of the graphics to load.)

6E: Choose one background (.gif or .jpeg) you would like to use in your Web page.

Hint! There are more subdirectories or folders containing additional backgrounds at this site. Scroll to the bottom of the page to see them.

Note: Backgrounds are graphics also, and can be saved using the same procedure you used in Step 3 above.

6F: Point to the background you want and click your right mouse button. (Hold the button down on Macintosh computers.)

6G: Save your background graphics as you did in Step 3.

Step 7: Return to the *HTML Activities Web Page.* Browse any of the other links that interest you in Activity 15. Visit and download any interesting graphics you find and save them in your **graphics** folder.

Creating a New Web page with a Background Image and a Graphic

Step 8: It is time to see if the graphics you downloaded really have a thousand words to say. To create a basic Web page with a background and a single graphic:

8A: Exit your Web browser and load your HTML Editor. If you are using a simple text editor, enter the beginning or starting tags as you did in Activity 1:

```
<HTML>
<HEAD><TITLE> </TITLE></HEAD>
<BODY>
</BODY>
</HTML>
```

8B: Insert the title, <TITLE>A Thousand Words</TITLE>.

8C: Insert the background attribute in the body tag as explained below:

Enter the name of the folder and graphic you want to use as your background value. The folder and graphic name are entered between quotation marks following the = sign without any spaces. The folder name **graphic** is in lowercase.

Note: A slash separates the folder from the name of the graphic. In the example below, the XXXXXXX is for the name of the graphic you selected. The ??? is the name of the file extension for your graphic, either .gif or .jpg.

```
</HEAD>
<BODY BACKGROUND="graphics/XXXXXXXX.???">
```

8D: Insert <H1><I> Getting the .gif of the Page</I> </H1> after the <BODY> tag.

8E: Type <HR ALIGN="LEFT" WIDTH = 75% SIZE = 10> under the <H1> tag.

8F: Insert a Paragraph break <P> after the line created in Step 8E.

8G: Insert your Web graphic (.gif or .jpg) under the <P> tag. It could be one of the graphics you found on the Web or one you created, but it must be located in the **graphics** folder you created.

<IMG SRC="graphics/XXXXXXXX.???">

8H: Your code should look similar to the code below:

```
<HTML>
<HEAD>
<TITLE>A Thousand Words</TITLE>
</HEAD>
<BODY BACKGROUND="graphics/XXXXXXXX.???">
<BODY>
<H1><I>Getting the .gif of the Page</I></H1>
<HR ALIGN="LEFT" WIDTH=75% SIZE=10>
<P>
<IMG SRC="graphics/XXXXXXXX.???">
</BODY>
</HTML>
```

If your code is correct, save your file in the **projects** directory or folder with the name **act15.htm** or **act15.html**.

Step 9: Start your Internet browser and open the file **act15.htm** or **act15.html**. See if your background and graphic have displayed correctly. If not, start troubleshooting as explained below.

Troubleshooting

If your page is having problems, check the following:

- Is the page saved in the **projects** directory or folder?
- Are the graphics saved in the **graphics** subdirectory in the **projects** folder?
- Did you insert file names rather than xxxxxx?
- Do all of your background and other graphic file names end in either .jpg or .gif?
- Are the file names in your HTML document spelled correctly?
- Did you position your quotation marks properly?
- Did you leave any spaces in the value definition?

After you have your page working, continue with the next step.

Step 10: Return to your editor and add more to this Web page. Be creative. Add new graphics and text to make an interesting page. For example, is your graphic too big? You may want to use the HEIGHT= and WIDTH= attributes as explained in Activity 9 to make your graphic smaller.

Debriefing

Graphics are an exciting way to make your page interesting and noteworthy. Repeat this exercise using Internet Assistant for Word. With Internet Assistant, adding backgrounds and graphics is really very easy.

1. Start a new HTML document by selecting **File**, **New**, then **Html.dot** from the **New** dialog box as outlined in Activity 12.

2. Save your document as **act15ia.htm** by selecting **Save As** from the **File** pull-down menu.

3. Select **Background and Links** from the **Format** menu.

4. Select the name of the background you want to use by clicking the **Browse** button and searching for your background graphic file in the **graphics** folder.

5. Select a graphic by clicking the **Picture** button or by selecting **picture** from the **Insert** pull-down menu.

6. Save your file again as **act15ia.htm**.

7. View your creation in your Web browser!

Extension: If you have time, try the following:

- Practice downloading graphics, icons, and images from different sites.
- Insert these images into your Web page.
- Change the background and see how your page changes.
- Learn how to make a picture bigger or smaller with Internet Assistant for Word. Remember to use the Help feature!

inking to Anchors

"Do you know what is cool about books? You can jump from page 42 to page 73 easily by flipping through the pages with your thumb. If you come to a long Web page, you may have to push the down arrow on the scroll bar for ages to see the bottom of the page."

In a book, you would use an index or a table of contents to list the important information in the book. In HTML, you can link within your document using internal hypertext links. These kinds of links are called by several names:

- Internal links
- Internal references
- Internal anchors
- Jumps

"As I have investigated the Net, I have seen at least five ways of organizing a Web page:"

1. Alphabetized lists (A, B, C, etc...)

2. Graphics (Interesting pictures take you to important places on the page)

3. Numbered lists (1, 2, 3, etc...)

4. Unordered lists (•, •, •, etc...)

5. Chronological lists (1901, 1902, 1903, etc...)

"Let's create a small document with a few chronological jumps in it. This will give you a feeling for how internal anchors work."

"The Olympics have always been a favorite subject of mine. Remember Activities 12, 13, and 14? To add to this collection of Olympic pages, I thought we could create a page titled "Where Have the Olympics Been?" Using internal anchors from a menu, we can access each of the years for 1950 to the year 2002."

Table of Tags for Activity 16		
Internal Links	<A HREF="#XXX"></A>	Internally links different parts of your HTML document. (Replace the XXX with a key word.)
Internal Anchors	<A NAME="XXX"></A>	Internal anchors create jumps in your HTML document. (Replace the XXX with a key word.)
Font Size	<FONT SIZE=+#></FONT>	Font Size lets you control the size of letters and text.

 Activity 16 Creating an Organized Layout

Objectives:

- Insert tags into an existing document.
- Convert a text file into an HTML document.
- Create Internal Anchors to parts of your Web page.
- Display menus for the Web surfer to use.
- Demonstrate the ability to create user-friendly Web pages.

Step 1: Start your Internet browser and load the *HTML Activities Web Page*.

> **http://www.thomson.com/swpco/internet/markweb.html**

Step 2: Locate <u>Activity 16: Linking to Anchors</u> from the Activity List menu.

Step 3: Click the <u>Olympic Sites File</u> from the *HTML Activities Web Page*.

Note: This is a text file that contains information regarding where the Winter Olympics have been held during the past 50 years.

3A: Click on any of the words inside the <u>Olympic Sites File</u>.

3B: Select **Save As** or **Save As File** from the **File** menu.

3C: Save the file to your **projects** folder naming it **olympic.txt**.

3D: If you were able to successfully save the file to your **projects** folder, jump to Step 4. If you are unable to find, open, or save the file **olympic.txt**, open SimpleText for Macintosh or Notepad for Windows and type the following information:

Where have the Winter Olympics Been?

The years 1950 to 2000

Winter Games

1950
| VI | Oslo, Norway |
| VII | Cortina, Italy |

1960
VIII	Squaw Valley, California, USA
IX	Innsbruck, Austria
X	Grenoble, France

1970
| XI | Sapporo, Japan |
| XII | Innsbruck, Austria |

1980
XIII	Lake Placid, New York, USA
XIV	Sarajevo, Yugoslavia
XV	Calgary, Alberta, Canada

```
1990
XVI      Albertville, France
XVII     Lillehammer, Norway
XVIII    Nagano, Japan

2000
XIX      Salt Lake City, Utah, USA
```

3E: After you have typed this information into your text editor, save it in your **projects** folder with the file name **olympic.txt**.

Step 4:
To create Internal Anchors or Jumps:

4A: Open SimpleText for Macintosh or Notepad for Windows.

4B: Select **File**, **Open** from the pull-down menu.

4C: Open the file **olympic.txt** from your **projects** folder.

Are you ready to Jump around?

Step 5:
To convert **olympic.txt** from a text document to an HTML document that your Web browser can read:

5A: Choose **File**, **Save As** from your pull-down menu.

5B: Select the **projects** directory or folder.

5C: Rename the document **olymyear.htm** or **olymyear.html**.

> **Hint!** Remember, if you are on a Macintosh or Windows 95 system you may use the longer file name extension .html.

5D: Save the document.

Step 6:
Begin creating an HTML document by inserting the basic tags within your text as follows:

6A: Insert the <HTML> tag at the beginning and the </HTML> tag at the end of this document.

6B: Don't forget the <HEAD><TITLE></TITLE></HEAD> tags right after the <HTML> tag.

6C: Key the title THE WINTER OLYMPIC YEARS between the <TITLE> tags.

6D: Insert the open <BODY> and close </BODY> tags in the appropriate places in the document. (If you forget where they go, review Activities 1, 2, and 4.)

> **Hint:** Insert the <BODY> tag just before the line "Where have the Winter Olympics Been?". Don't forget the </BODY> close tag at the end of the document.

6E: Place the background attribute within the open body tag. Use one of the images you downloaded in Activity 15 as the attribute as shown here. Replace the XXXXXXX and ??? between the quotation marks with the file name of the image:
<BODY BACKGROUND="XXXXXXX.???">

6F: Insert the format tags <B><I><FONT SIZE=+3> above the first line of the document that reads "Where have the Winter Olympics Been?" Make sure you turn off each of these tags with the appropriate close tags, </B>, </I>, </FONT>.

6G: Insert the heading tags, <H2></H2> for the text "The years 1950 to 2002" and "Winter Games."

6H: Each of the section headings — 1950, 1960, 1970, 1980, 1990, and 2000 — should have the tags <H4> and <B>. (Be sure to turn them off also with </H4> and </B> tags.)

6I: Italicize the information under each of the decades.

6J: Insert a Break tag <BR> at the end of each Olympic site and a <P> tag between the years.

6K: Your document should look like the example in Figure A16-1. Make any corrections you need to make.

How are we doing so far?

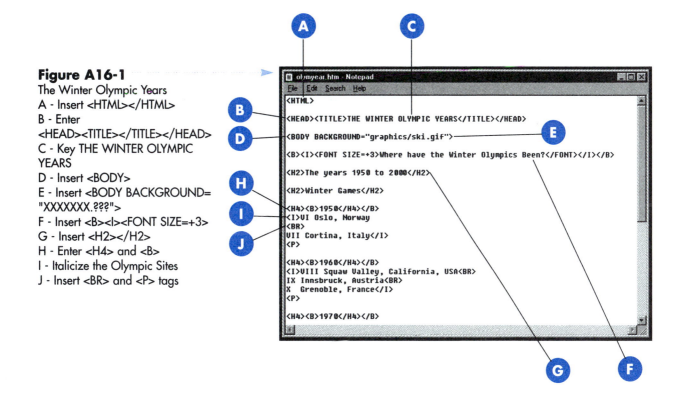

Figure A16-1

The Winter Olympic Years
A - Insert <HTML></HTML>
B - Enter <HEAD><TITLE></TITLE></HEAD>
C - Key THE WINTER OLYMPIC YEARS
D - Insert <BODY>
E - Insert <BODY BACKGROUND="XXXXXXX.???">
F - Insert <B><I><FONT SIZE=+3>
G - Insert <H2></H2>
H - Enter <H4> and <B>
I - Italicize the Olympic Sites
J - Insert <BR> and <P> tags

Making the Links

Time to create hypertext links and anchors within your Web page. These links will create a menu that Web surfers can use to move conveniently around your Web page.

Step 7: Create links to the different decades of the page from 1950 - 2000.

7A: Position your cursor under the words "Winter Games."

7B: Insert a reference link as follows with a space and an extra slash as shown in Figure A16-2:

`<A HREF="#1950">1950</A> /`

Drop the Anchor

Now we're going to create the anchor for the links to find:

Step 8: Insert the following anchor tag for each year in the **olympic.htm** file as shown in Figure A16-2:

`<A NAME = "1950"></A>`

Hint! Make sure the 1950 in the NAME tag is identical to the 1950 in the HREF= # tag.

Figure A16-2
Creating Internal Links
A - Position your cursor
B - Insert <A HREF= "#XXXX">XXXX</A> /
C - <A NAME = "XXXX"></A>

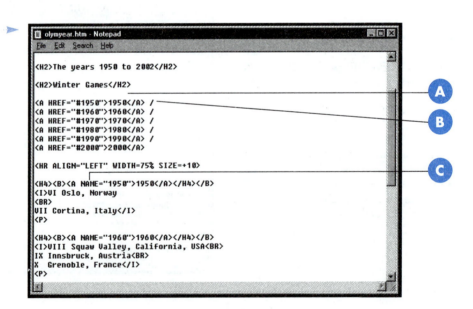

Step 9: Redo Steps 7 and 8 for each of the decades of your document. Be careful to change the years as you go from decade to decade.

Hint! You can use the Copy and Paste features to make things go faster.

Step 10: Create the <HR ALIGN="LEFT" WIDTH=75% SIZE=+2> tag after the last decade link in your menu at the beginning of the document. This will create a separation bar between the menu and the first decade section as shown in Figure A16-2.

Step 11:

Your page should be ready to view and try out. Save your work before you exit your text editor, then view your creation in your Web browser. Your page should look like the one shown in Figure A16-3.

Figure A16-3
The Winter Olympic Years
Internal Links by Decade

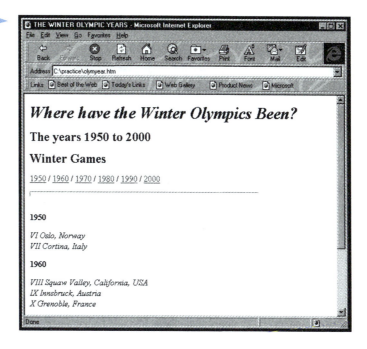

Troubleshooting

If your page is having problems, try and debug the Olympic Web page yourself. Look for the following:

• Have you used the SAME names for the Anchors and the Links?
• Have you checked the code for spelling errors or tag errors or missing <BRACKETS>?
• Have a friend read the code and see if they can locate any errors.

Extension:

1. You now have a menu and internal anchors for each of the decades of your page. However, once you have moved down to the decade, you may need to scroll back to the top of the page to select another decade! Outrageous! This is entirely too much work.

   Here is a problem for you to solve. Figure out how to put a link at the bottom of the page that will take you right to the top of the page. Name this link To The Top.

2. If you have time, try the following:

   • Insert bars, graphics, and icons into the page

   • Center portions of the text

   • Find and insert graphics into the document

   • Insert text about the Olympic sites

   • Locate hypertext links to the Olympic cities

3. Word users can create internal links very easily. Try this additional activity using Word's Internet Assistant:

   a. Visit the *HTML Activities Web Page.*

   b. Click on the <u>Glossary</u> Link.

   c. Save a copy of the Glossary to your **projects** folder as you learned to do earlier in this lesson. Name it **glossary.txt**.

   d. Open the **glossary.txt** file using Internet Assistant for Word. To make it an HTML file, click **File, Save As**, then name the file **glossary.htm**.

   e. Key the letters of the alphabet along the top of the glossary as shown in Figure A16-4. Place a slash between each letter. Leave spaces between the letters and the slashes.

   f. Scroll down to the word that matches the letter in your alphabetic list. In Figure A16-4, the first C word has been selected for this example. Highlight the word by clicking and dragging your mouse over the word.

   g. Click the **Bookmark** button or select **Bookmark** from the **Edit** pull-down menu.

   h. Enter the letter you are bookmarking.

   i. Click **Add**.

Figure A16-4

Creating Bookmarks
f - Select your word
g - Click Bookmark button
h - Enter the letter
i - Click Add

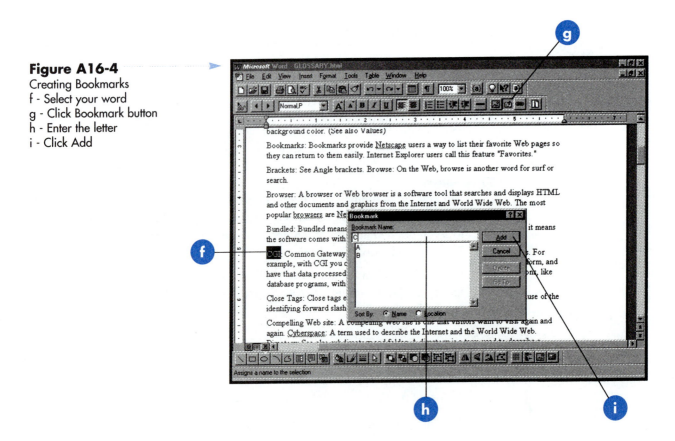

4. Once you have created all the bookmarks needed for the alphabetic list, create the internal links.

    j. Select the letter you are linking. In Figure A16-5, the letter C has been selected.

    k. Click the **Hyperlink** button as shown in Figure A16-5 or select **Hyperlink** from the **Insert** menu.

    l. Click the **Bookmark location in file** option down arrow.

    m. Select the letter you are linking.

    n. Press **OK**.

    o. Test the links by double-clicking on them. They should jump to the first word in the glossary with the letter you have indicated.

    p. Open your Web browser and try your glossary. How does it work?

    q. Return to your text file **olympic.htm** and enter internal links that will take you from the end of each section of words to the top of the page again. For example, at the end of the C words, create a link called Glossary that takes you back to your alphabetic list.

Figure A16-5

Creating Internal Links
j - Select the letter
k - Click Hyperlink button
l - Click Bookmark location in file down arrow
m - Select the letter you need
n - Click OK

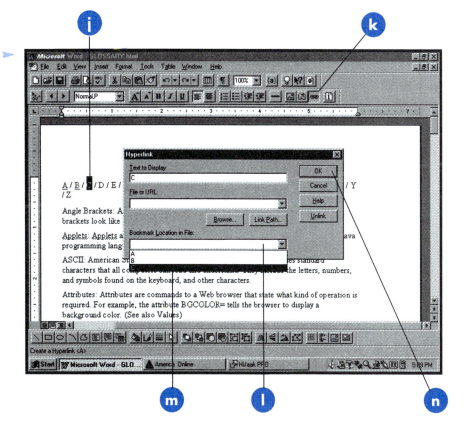

Debriefing

Web pages can become long and complicated. Internal links help Web page readers find the information they are interested in without becoming frustrated by endless scrolling and searching.

Indexes can be created using alphabetized, numbered, unordered, or chronological lists. Pictures can also be used to link Web page readers to interesting parts of a Web page.

When you use hypertext to link to different parts of a single Web page, you are demonstrating that you have a good understanding of HTML commands and <TAGS>.

Three Pages in One

"Some Web browsers have a special Frames feature. This feature allows you to view more than one Web page at a time in a single Web browser window. I used Frames in my *HTML Activities Web Page*. Can you see the different frames in Figure A17-1?"

Top Frame for the Logo

Figure A17-1
The *HTML Activities Web Page* has three frames. Each frame has its own HTML Web page inside it.

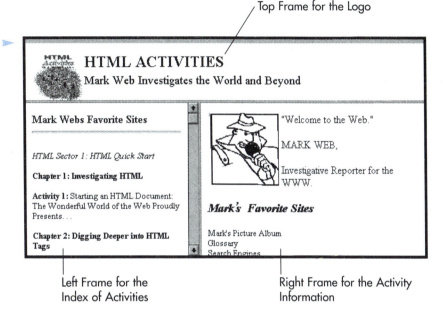

HTML ACTIVITIES
Mark Web Investigates the World and Beyond

Mark Webs Favorite Sites

HTML Sector 1: HTML Quick Start

Chapter 1: Investigating HTML

Activity 1: Starting an HTML Document: The Wonderful World of the Web Proudly Presents. . .

Chapter 2: Digging Deeper into HTML Tags

"Welcome to the Web."

MARK WEB,

Investigative Reporter for the WWW.

Mark's Favorite Sites

Mark's Picture Album
Glossary
Search Engines

Left Frame for the
Index of Activities

Right Frame for the Activity
Information

"The ability to display several Web pages at the same time could be an important part of your growing Web site. It is in mine. When you access my page, the browser window is divided into three areas or frames."

• The top frame is Mark Web's logo.
• The left frame is for the index that launches the activities.
• The right frame displays activity pages.

Frames can divide your browser screen into individual windows that load different HTML files. You may have two, three, four, or more HTML pages loaded at the same time. Frames create an interesting page, but you need to be aware of your audience when you create them. Some browsers may not be able to view frames; therefore, be selective when you use them.

In this activity, you'll be creating a Web page with three frames. To do this, you'll need to create *four* HTML files — one for each of the frames and another to pull the frames together into one Web page.

O b j e c t i v e s :

• Organize HTML documents into a workable display.
• Create a frame HTML document to display three HTML files.

Table of Tags for Activity 17

Frame Rows	<FRAMESET ROWS...>	Divides the browser window into horizontal frames.
Frame Columns	<FRAMESET COLS...>	Divides the browser window into vertical frames.
Turn Off Frame	</FRAMESET>	Used to turn off the Frame Settings.
Text Area	<BLOCKQUOTE>	Used to designate a block of text as a quote.
Loading URLs	TARGET="_top"	Used when you don't want to use frames to display the page.

To use the <FRAMESET> tag, there are a few additional things you should know:

- Frames are like multiple windows in the same browser. (See Figure A17-1.)
- Frames are named in a beginning or master document which accesses and loads other HTML pages.
- Frames are named in the master document so you can direct other pages to load into a specific frame. You will learn about target tags in this activity.
- Frames can be erased and you can load a new Web page using the target="_top" tag.
- Frames can be fun and creative.

It's time to build some frames! First we will create the top frame. Then, in Step 2 we'll create the left frame. Step 3 takes us through the creation of the right frame and Step 4 will help you create the master file that accesses the other documents.

Step 1: Open your HTML Editor and create the following document:

```
<HTML>
<HEAD>
<TITLE>TOP FRAME WINDOW</TITLE>
</HEAD>
<BODY>
<CENTER>
<FONT SIZE = +2><I>Welcome to</FONT><BR>
<FONT SIZE =+3>insert your name here Frames Page</FONT></I>
</CENTER>
</BODY>
</HTML>
```

Save the document in your **projects** directory with the file name **frtop.htm**. This will become the Top Frame page of your document.

Note: You can also name the files using the .html extension. If you do, be consistent and use .html for all the files and in every link.

To create your left frame:

2A: Start a new HTML document and enter the following tags to create a second HTML page to use in your left frame:

```
<HTML>
<HEAD>
<TITLE>My Links</TITLE>
</HEAD>
<BODY BACKGROUND="graphics/XXXXXXXX.???">
<BODY>
<I><FONT SIZE =+2>My Favorite Links on the Web</FONT></I>
<P>
```

Create 10 hypertext links to your favorite sites on the Internet. (Refer to Activity 5.) Insert a <BR> command between each link. The following is an example.

```
<A HREF="http://www.disney.com" target="_top">Disney Home
Page</A>
<BR>
</BODY>
</HTML>
```

You will notice that in the <A HREF=""> above we have added target="_ top". This is important. Let's take a few minutes and talk about the target tag:

• If you would like to update the entire browser window, you can use target="_top". Regardless of the current frames, the entire window will be updated to the new Web page.

```
<A HREF="http://www.Disney.com" target = "_ Top"> Disney Home
Page </A>
```

• When we create the master document, we will name each of the frames. Using the target tag, you can have the new page load in another window of your choosing. If the top window were named topframe, you could use the tag target="_topframe". This would load a new document in the top frame and leave the others the same.

```
<A HREF="http://www.Disney.com" target = "_TopFrame"> Disney
Home Page </A>
```

• If you leave a target out, the page will load in the same frame as the hypertext link. All the other pages in the frame stay the same, and only the one frame will change.

```
<A HREF="http://www.Disney.com"> Disney Home Page </A>
```

Later, when you have some time, try the different parts of the target tag. For now, we are going to use target="_top" to update the entire window.

2B: Save the file as **frleft.htm** in your **projects** directory.

This page will be accessed by the Left Side of your document.

Step 3:   For the third page, create an HTML document informing the Web surfer about the city you live in. Use the appropriate tags, tell about your city, give any hypertext references linking back to your city, and give other sites to visit that may be of interest. If you need help, please review the activities you have completed thus far (The Web page you created in Activity 6 may come in handy here.)

When you are finished, save the file as **frright.htm** in your **projects** directory. Your document will load this page on the Right Side.

Now that you have created the three needed documents, you are ready to create the tags to access them into a framed browser screen.

Step 4:   Start a new HTML document and create the frames page:

The Frameset Rows tag will set the horizontal spacing of the frames. The Frameset Cols will set the vertical size of the frames. By changing these numbers, you can change the size of each of your frames.

Key the following tags in your HTML Editor:

```
<HTML>
<HEAD>

<TITLE>Insert your name here Frames Page</TITLE>
<FRAMESET ROWS="100,80%" NAME="Welcome">
<FRAME SRC="frtop.htm" SCROLLING=NO>
        <FRAMESET COLS="200,270">
                <FRAME SRC="frleft.htm" NAME="frleft.htm">
                <FRAME SRC="frright.htm" NAME="frright.htm">
        </FRAMESET>
</FRAMESET>

</HEAD>

<BODY>

<BLOCKQUOTE>
Welcome to my Frames Page. This page has been enhanced with
Frames Tags. If you are not seeing the frames, you need to use a
frame-capable browser to see my page. Please visit my page again
when you have loaded a frame-capable browser.
</BLOCKQUOTE>

</BODY>

</HTML>
```

Read the code and see if you can find what each of the three frames were named. Did you find WELCOME, LEFT, and RIGHT? You can name the frames whatever you like, but it is much easier to relate the names to the page you are working on or to the placement of the frame.

Note: The <BLOCKQUOTE> you inserted informs Web surfers who cannot view frames that they have accessed a frame page. You should inform your visitor that you do have a frame page and they will need to use a frame-capable browser before they will be able to view your page.

When you are finished, save this file in the **projects** directory with the name **frmain.htm**. You are ready to view your page and see if your links are functioning correctly.

→ Step 5: Exit your HTML Editor and load your Internet browser. Choose **File — Open File**. Change to your **projects** directory and select the file **frmain.htm**.

Your frames should be working great. If your page isn't working, refer to the troubleshooting section below.

Troubleshooting

If you are having problems, review the following:

• Check your codes in all four documents for spelling, link, case, or tagging errors.
• Are all your files in the same directory, like the **projects** folder?
• Are all your graphics in the correct folder, like the **graphics** folder?
• Can your browser read frames?

Extension: If you have time, try the following:

• Experiment using graphics.

• Create links to access other pages you have created.

• Change the target tag to "right" or "welcome" and see if you can activate different frames of the page.

Debriefing

Frames are a great way to grab the attention of the Web surfer. When Web users visit your page, you can grab their attention quickly if you have placed your frames correctly. If you don't like the way your frames look, go back and change the ROWS and COL numbers in the **frmain.htm** page and then view them again. Get it the way you want others to see it on the Web.

Here are my official HTML notes for Activity 17:

1. Frames divide the Web page into parts determined by the creator of the page.

2. Each of the frames can display a different HTML document at the same time.

3. Not all browsers can view frames.

Setting Your Table on the Net

Tables are another great way to organize and display information. Tables are wonderful. They help you organize and display information in a neat — or is that NET? — way.

When you create a table, you organize your information into cells. There are many sites out on the Net that give you the opportunity to view and use tables. Here is an example of one of them.

Figure A18-1:
A Calendar Created as a Table

Monthly Calendar						
Sun	Mon	Tues	Wed	Thur	Fri	Sat
1	2	3	4	5	6	
7	8	9	10	11	12	13
14	15	16	17	18	19	20
21	22	23	24	25	26	27
28	29	30	31			

Rows

Columns

In this activity, you will create a Web page that includes a table. You will also change different parts of the table to add variety, ease of access, and appeal.

Creating a table is like using a spreadsheet program or using a table to display information in a word processor. It is a combination of rows and columns. In a spreadsheet, **rows** represent the horizontal information, while **columns** represent the vertical information. The box that is created is called a **cell**.

NOTE: Don't get these rows and columns confused with the rows and columns you just learned in Activity 17 on Frames. They are similar, but used very differently.

Tables on the Web have **rows** to divide information into groups, and **columns** to divide the groups into parts, much the same as a spreadsheet. In fact, the following is a table with rows and columns!

Activity 18 Informational Pages

Table of Tags for Activity 18		
Beginning and Ending Table Tags	<TABLE> </TABLE>	These tags begin and end the table.
Table Title	<CAPTION> </CAPTION>	Similar to the <TITLE> tag, only creates a "title" for the table.
Create Rows	<TR></TR>	Table Row <TR> tags are used to create rows in the table.
Divide Rows into Columns	<TH></TH>	Table Headings <TH> divide rows into columns and describe each column of the table.
Table Data	<TD></TD>	Actual data of each cell of the table.

In this activity, we're going to create a Web table that lists teachers, the classes they teach, and their classrooms.

O b j e c t i v e s :

- Learn the tags necessary to create a table using HTML.
- Create several tables, adjusting the settings to view different options.
- Display your table in a Web browser.

Step 1: Load your HTML Editor.

Step 2: Begin a new Web page.

Step 3: Enter the basic starting tags. (See Activity 1 if you need help.)

Step 4: Insert a title and a background into your Web page.

    4A: Enter **Teachers on the Net** for the title of this Web page.

    4B: Insert the tag for an appropriate background. If you saved your background images from Activity 15 in the **graphics** directory, your tag will look like the following:

        <BODY BACKGROUND="graphics/XXXXXXXX.???">

Step 5: On the line below the <BODY> tag, enter the following tag and text:

        <H1>HTML Internet High School</H1><P>

Step 6: Position your cursor under the tag created in Step 5 and press Return several times to add space for you to type your <TABLE> tags.

Step 7: Position the cursor two lines below the "HTML Internet High School" line and type the following tags and text. If your HTML Editor creates tables automatically, use the feature to create these tags.

```
<TABLE BORDER>
<CAPTION>Classes by Teacher</CAPTION>
    <TR>
        <TH>TEACHER</TH>
        <TH>CLASS</TH>
    <TH>CYBER ROOM NUMBER</TH>
    </TR>
    <TR>
        <TD>CORY BARKSDALE</TD>
        <TD>COMPUTER MATH</TD>
        <TD>212</TD>
    </TR>
    <TR>
        <TD>MICHELLE ANNE</TD>
        <TD>PHYSICAL EDUCATION</TD>
        <TD>GYM 1</TD>
    </TR>
    <TR>
        <TD>MARI KATHLEEN</TD>
        <TD>LIFE/SOCIAL SKILLS</TD>
        <TD>115</TD>
    </TR>
    <TR>
        <TD>JENNIFER PAULSEN</TD>
        <TD>HOME ECONOMICS</TD>
        <TD>125</TD>
    </TR>
  <TR>
        <TD>THOMAS HAROLD</TD>
        <TD>FOOTBALL COACH</TD>
        <TD>GYM2</TD>
    </TR>
  <TR>
        <TD>KATE ELIZABETH</TD>
        <TD>DRAMA</TD>
        <TD>225</TD>
    </TR>
</TABLE>
```

Step 8: Save the file in your **projects** directory as **table1.htm** or **table1.html.**

Step 9: Close your HTML Editor and load your Web browser.

Step 10: View the file you just created. When your file loads, your table should look similar to the one in Figure A18-2. If you do not see a table similar to the one on the next page, then your browser may not support tables.

Figure A18-2
A Web Page that
Contains a Table

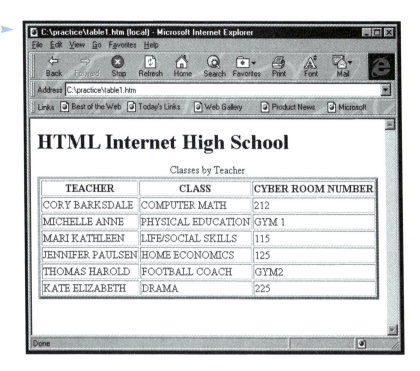

C:\practice\table1.htm (local) - Microsoft Internet Explorer

File Edit View Go Favorites Help

Back Forward Stop Refresh Home Search Favorites Print Font Mail

Address C:\practice\table1.htm

Links Best of the Web Today's Links Web Gallery Product News Microsoft

HTML Internet High School

Classes by Teacher

TEACHER	CLASS	CYBER ROOM NUMBER
CORY BARKSDALE	COMPUTER MATH	212
MICHELLE ANNE	PHYSICAL EDUCATION	GYM 1
MARI KATHLEEN	LIFE/SOCIAL SKILLS	115
JENNIFER PAULSEN	HOME ECONOMICS	125
THOMAS HAROLD	FOOTBALL COACH	GYM2
KATE ELIZABETH	DRAMA	225

Done

Complete the following steps to add a 3-D effect to the table:

Step 11: Reload **table1.htm** into your HTML Editor.

11A: Locate the tag <TABLE BORDER>. Add the value = 4 to the tag as follows:

<TABLE BORDER = 4 >

Hint! Play with the table border values. Try 10 or 20! See what happens.

11B: Click the **File** menu and choose **Save As**. Save your file as **table2.htm** or **table2.html**.

11C: Reload your Web browser and load the file **table2.htm**.

Can you identify the change? The addition of = 4 created a different look to your Web page by increasing the size of the border around your table.

Troubleshooting

If your table is not working properly, have you:

• Checked your browser to make sure it can read tables?
• Rechecked your tags for correct placement and accuracy of tags?
• Located all tags necessary to create tables as outlined?

Debriefing

In this activity, you created a simple table with basic tags. Using tables will help organize and display information for those who visit your Web page.

Tables are very easy to create in Internet Assistant for Word:

1. Start Word.

2. Create a new HTML document by selecting **File**, **New**, then **HTML.dot** from the **New** dialog box as explained in Activity 12.

3. Save your document as **act18ia.htm** by selecting **Save As** from the **File** pull-down menu.

4. Select the **Insert Rows** button as shown in Figure A18-3.

5. Select as many rows and columns as you need for your table.

6. Enter information into the table by clicking your mouse and typing in each field of the table.

That's all there is to it! Remember to save your work before you exit.

Figure A18-3
Create Tables in Internet Assistant for Word
4 - Click the Insert Rows button
5 - Select your Rows and Columns

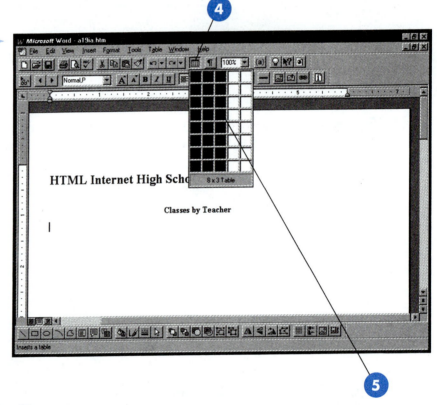

Extension:

1. If you want to extend your experience, try the following, using your **table2.htm** file:

- Add graphics to the page.
- Add hypertext links inside the cells to your teacher's Web page.
- Create a bar to divide the table information from other parts of the page.

2. Now that you know how easy it is to create a table in Word, create a table that compares things. For example, compare the burgers at three fast food restaurants. Create rows and columns. Include a column for the name of the burger and a column for the price. Create a column for ingredients.

What Do You Need to Know?

"You've already learned about two layout tools, frames and tables. In this activity, you will learn how to collect information using the HTML forms feature."

"Collecting information is as important as sharing information over the Net. Businesses, schools, and government agencies want to know more about those who visit their Web sites. Web forms allow Web sites to gather all kinds of information, like names, favorite restaurants, bank account numbers, credit card numbers, favorite music CDs, top ten TV shows, or best computer games."

There are several different types of forms and form tools you will learn about in Activities 19 and 20:

1. Text fields or text area boxes (Activity 19)
2. Radio buttons (Activity 19)
3. Check boxes (Activity 20)

Table of Tags for Activity 19

Beginning and Ending Form Tags	<FORM METHOD></FORM>	These tags are used to begin and end the Forms section of your HTML document. Other tags for Radio buttons, Check boxes, and Lists can be inserted between these tags.
Type of Input Requested	<INPUT TYPE>	Defines the type of input allowed for the tag you are using.
Text Field	<INPUT TYPE="TEXT"	Defines the type of input or text information to be inserted.
Identifies the Field	NAME=" "	Displays prompt words on the browser screen.
Defines Size of Input Cell	SIZE=" "	Defines the size of the input area for text to be entered.
Radio Buttons	<INPUT TYPE="RADIO"	Displays a list of choices, with a selection button for each. Only one choice can be made.

O b j e c t i v e s :

*   Visit selected sites on the Web that use forms.
*   Create a form with text boxes and radio buttons.
*   View and use the form you create in your Web browser.

Forms Field Trip

Step 1: To start this activity, let's take an Internet field trip and view several Web sites that use forms to gather information.

1A: Start your Web browser and load the *HTML Activities Web Page*. Click the ACTIVITY 19 Form Design hypertext link.

1B: Locate the heading "Field Trip of Forms." There are several links in this section to visit. Let's take a few minutes and visit several of these sites.

1C: Choose the Campbell Soup link. We are going to look for recipes using Campbell's soup.

These forms direct the users to qualify their choices. Each choice is directed by the Web page, not the user. Locate a recipe with the following information:

- Click the down arrow on the **Courses** menu and choose **Main Dishes**.
- Click the down arrow on the **Recipe Type** menu and choose **One Dish**.
- Click the down arrow on the **Ingredient** menu and choose Chicken/Turkey.
- Click the down arrow on the **Campbell's Brand/Products** menu and choose **Campbell's® Cream of Mushroom Soup** (or another soup if you find Cream of Mushroom totally disgusting.)

1D: Click the **Search** button to find a list of recipes that matches your choices. The choices you made are really hypertext links to take you to the specific recipe. Choose one and see what you get.

Note: Notice how forms can help narrow a search for the Web user as they make choices based on the questions that are asked.

Hint! While you are here, you may want to print this recipe and any others you find, take them home, and cook a great dinner.

Step 2: Search engine form fields help Web surfers find information:

2A: Return to the *HTML Activities Web Page* and select a search engine.

2B: Enter the word INTERNET in the Keyword box and click the **Start Search** button.

Note: You should receive a message indicating the number of pages with the word INTERNET in the document title. See how simple forms can really help to collect information about Web pages. Instead of searching, the search engine helped you narrow the search down.

Hint! If you have extra time, you can visit other sites from the Activity 19 page. Each of these pages have forms that are used differently. If you are ready, it is time to write your own forms to post on the Web.

Create Your Own Form

If you were not able to participate in the field trip, your current browser may not be capable of viewing forms. Ask your instructor, or check your documentation, to find out if your browser is form capable. If it is not, you may want to load a form-capable browser before you continue with this activity.

For this activity, you are going to create a form page to gather information about students' likes and dislikes. Remember, never ask for full names or addresses.

Step 3: Start your text editor and begin a new Web page.

Step 4: Enter the following tags into your HTML Editor:

```
<HTML>
<HEAD>
<TITLE>Web Forms </TITLE>
</HEAD>
<BODY>

<CENTER>
<FONT SIZE=+5><I><B>My Web Form Page</B></I></FONT>
</CENTER>

<HR WIDTH=75% ALIGN="CENTER">

<H3>Please enter the following information:</H3>

<FORM METHOD="POST" ACTION="">
Enter your First Name:<INPUT TYPE="TEXT" NAME="FIRST NAME"
SIZE="20"><BR>
Enter the Name of your State:<INPUT TYPE="TEXT" NAME="STATE"
SIZE="20"><BR>
Enter your Postal Code:<INPUT TYPE="TEXT" NAME="POSTAL CODE"
SIZE="10"><P>

<HR>

The color I like most is:<BR>
<INPUT TYPE="RADIO" NAME="COLOR" VALUE="">Grassy Green<BR>
<INPUT TYPE="RADIO" NAME="COLOR" VALUE="">Sky Blue<BR>
<INPUT TYPE="RADIO" NAME="COLOR" VALUE="">Fire Engine
Red<BR>
<INPUT TYPE="RADIO" NAME="COLOR" VALUE="">Daisy Yellow<BR>
<INPUT TYPE="RADIO" NAME="COLOR" VALUE="">14-Karat Gold<P>

</FORM>
</BODY>
</HTML>
```

Step 5: Save this file in your **projects** directory with the file name **form19.htm** or **form19.html.**

Step 6: Close your text editor and load your Web browser. Open **form19.htm** from your **projects** folder.

Step 7: Your document should load into your browser and look similar to Figure A19-1.

Figure A19-1
Form Created in
Activity 19

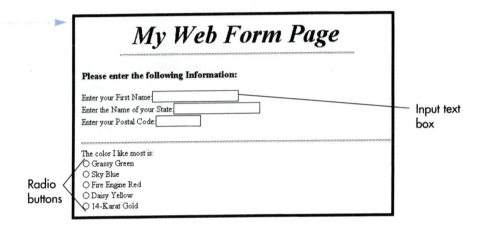

My Web Form Page

Please enter the following Information:

Enter your First Name:
Enter the Name of your State:
Enter your Postal Code:

Input text box

The color I like most is:
○ Grassy Green
○ Sky Blue
○ Fire Engine Red
○ Daisy Yellow
○ 14-Karat Gold

Radio buttons

Step 8: Try the form you created:

8A: Enter your name in the First Name box.

8B: Click the State box and enter your state.

8C: Click the Postal Code box and enter your postal code.

8D: Use your mouse and select one of your favorite colors.

> **Note:** The Radio Button will darken for your choice. Choose a different button and your first choice is erased. You can only choose one. Radio buttons should allow only one choice.

Troubleshooting

If your form is not working properly, try the following:
- As always, check the tags for spelling or symbol errors.
- Make sure you are loading a new copy of the file and not an old one cached on your hard drive.
- Have someone else look at your tags for any errors.

You will be using this file in the next activity, so for now, you may want to save your work and begin the next activity. If you do want to change the file, create a backup of the file to use in the next activity.

Debriefing

Input areas and Radio buttons are only two parts to the forms pages you can create. In the next activity, you will learn about Check boxes and Text boxes.

Here are my official HTML notes from this activity:

1. Forms are used to collect information from the Web for use by the Web page authors.

2. Input areas or text fields can vary in Type, Size, and Value.

3. You can select only one Radio button from a forms page.

4. Review the tags you created:

    <FORM METHOD="POST" ACTION="">

    The method will be to POST the information to the server. The ACTION is a required attribute to specify the destination of the page once it is submitted. This could either be a URL on a server or an e-mail address. We will leave the Action blank for now.

    <INPUT TYPE="TEXT" NAME="" SIZE="">

    This tag determines what the person will see in their Web browser window. The input type could be Text, Check box, Radio, Image, or Hidden. We will use some of these later. Name="" refers to what the contents of the box will be. Size="" sets a size for the text window.

    <INPUT TYPE="RADIO">

    This is the same as the "TEXT" input, only this will create a Radio button viewed in your browser window. Text that follows this tag, such as Sky Blue or Daisy Yellow, will be choices the viewer has to choose from. The Name="" names the contents of this field. Value="" specifies the value that will be submitted if the box is checked.

Click Yes, Click No, Click I Don't Know

Activity 19 introduced you to forms, including Radio buttons and Input boxes. In this activity, you will learn about another forms tool called check boxes.

Radio buttons, like those created in the previous activity, only allow one choice. Check boxes allow for multiple answers. When it is necessary to choose "ALL that apply" instead of only one answer, check boxes are the solution.

Figure 20-1
Check Boxes Allow
Multiple Answers

Enter your First Name:
Enter the Name of your State:
Enter your Postal Code:

The color I like most is:
○ Grassy Green
○ Sky Blue
○ Fire Engine Red
○ Daisy Yellow
○ 14-Karat Gold

Click ALL that apply:
Check Boxes
☐ I like summer
☐ I like to ski
☐ I am taller than 5 feet
☐ I have a job
☐ I have never got an "F" in school
☐ I have a pet

Being able to use the different tags effectively adds appeal and uniqueness to your Web page layout. You can add even more appeal by learning how to use other input tools, such as:

- Selection lists
- Text boxes
- Submit and Reset buttons

Table of Tags for Activity 20		
Check box Field in Forms	<INPUT TYPE= "CHECKBOX"	Type of input used in the Web page. This will create a Check box.
Selection List	<SELECT NAME= " "	Begins a Selection list of possible choices.
Selection Choice	<OPTION>	Gives a choice for the Selection list.
Written Text Field	<TEXTAREA NAME	Creates a text area. TYPE, COLS, ROWS contained in the tag are explained in the activity.
Submit Information	<INPUT TYPE= "SUBMIT"	Creates a button to submit information to the destination designated in ACTION.
Reset Information	<INPUT TYPE= "RESET"	Resets the forms page back to default.

Activity **20** Checking the Boxes

O b j e c t i v e s :

- Load the file from Activity 19.
- Add Check box and Text area tags.
- Use a Selection list to gather information.
- Create Submit and Reset buttons.
- Determine the usefulness of forms on the Web.

Step 1:

Load your HTML Editor and retrieve the file **form19.htm** from your **projects** directory. This is the file you saved in Activity 19. Insert the following tags and text between the last line of the Radio button tag (<INPUT TYPE="RADIO" NAME="COLOR" VALUE="">14-Karat Gold<P>).

<INPUT TYPE="RADIO" NAME="COLOR" VALUE="">14-Karat Gold<P>

<HR>

Click ALL that apply:
<INPUT TYPE="CHECKBOX" VALUE="">I like summer
<INPUT TYPE="CHECKBOX" VALUE="">I like to ski
<INPUT TYPE="CHECKBOX" VALUE="">I am taller than 5 feet
<INPUT TYPE="CHECKBOX" VALUE="">I have a job
<INPUT TYPE="CHECKBOX" VALUE="">I have never got an "F" in school
<INPUT TYPE="CHECKBOX" VALUE="">I have a pet<P>

</FORM>

Step 2:

Review the document for spelling or tagging errors.

Step 3:

Save your file using the following steps:

3A: Choose **File, Save As**. (Make sure you choose SAVE AS because you are going to change the name of the file.)

3B: Save the file in your **projects** directory with the file name **form20.htm** or **form20.html**.

Step 4:

View your forms in your Web browser. Locate **form20.htm** or **form20.html** in your **projects** directory. Test your form by clicking in several of the Check boxes. Do they all work?

Note: Can you select more than one? Can you de-select a Check box once you have chosen it? Identify the difference between your Radio buttons and Check boxes. You should be able to choose several Check boxes, but only one Radio button.

"It's great to see your Web page developing and beginning to take shape. However, we are not through yet!"

Creating a Selection List

In the next set of steps, you will be creating a list of food items a person can choose from. Just like with a menu, you are giving the viewer a choice of items.

Step 5: Close your browser, return to your HTML Editor, and load the file **form20.htm** or **form20.html**. Position your cursor two lines under the last Check box tags, but before the </FORM> tag.

Step 6: Enter the following line of text and tags:

<INPUT TYPE ="CHECKBOX" VALUE="">I have a pet<P>

```
<HR>
What is your Favorite Food?<BR>
<SELECT NAME="Type of Food">
    <OPTION SELECTED>Pizza
    <OPTION>Hamburgers and Fries
    <OPTION>Deluxe Tacos
    <OPTION>Hot Lasagna
    <OPTION>Bar-b-Que Chicken
    <OPTION>Bean Burritos
    <OPTION>Prime Rib Steak
</SELECT><P>
```

</FORM>

Step 7: Review the document for spelling or tagging errors.

Step 8: Choose **File**, **Save** on the menu bar. (The file name should still be **form20.htm**.)

Step 9: Test your creation. Close your HTML Editor and load your Web browser. Locate **form20.htm** or **form20.html** in your **projects** directory. Scroll down to the Selection List section you just entered. It looks like an Input block with the word "Pizza" selected. Click the arrow key on the right side and the selection list will pop up. Choose one of the words from the list by clicking it with your mouse pointer.

Creating Text Boxes

One last item you should add to your forms page is a text box. This is an area designated for written text by the person viewing your page. The other items on the form page create a forced answer; however, the text box is an area where the person can put their own information.

Step 10: Close your Web browser and load your text editor.

Step 11: Open the file **form20.htm** or **form20.html** from the **projects** directory.

Step 12: Locate the area above the </FORM> tag and insert the following tags and text:

    <HR>

    Enter the name of your School Below
    <TEXTAREA NAME="WORDS" TYPE="TEXT" COLS=35 ROWS=2>
    This is a good place
    To add unique information
      </TEXTAREA>

Step 13: Review the document for spelling or tagging errors.

Creating Submit and Reset Buttons

After all of the information is gathered, there must be a way for the viewer to send, or submit, the information. The Submit tag and the Reset tag are the last two tags we need to create on this page.

Step 14: Enter the following tags just above the </FORM> tag and after the </TEXTAREA> tag you just finished:

    </TEXTAREA>
    <HR>
    <INPUT TYPE="SUBMIT" VALUE="Submit Information">
    <INPUT TYPE="RESET" VALUE="Reset Forms Page">
    </FORM>

Step 15: Review the document for spelling or tagging errors.

Step 16: Save your file again and view your changes in your Web browser. Did everything work?

Note: Take a minute and look at what you have created. Check the different form elements. Scroll down to the bottom of your document and try the pop-up Selection list. Enter the name of your school in the text box. Try out the Reset Forms Page. Does the information you checked and added in your form page erase?

Troubleshooting

If you are having trouble with your page, try the following:
- Check your tags for errors like missing " " or brackets < >.
- Have a friend look at your tags and offer suggestions.
- Check your tags with form20.htm link from the Activity 20 Web page.

Extension: If you have time, try some of these ideas:
- Create additional Check boxes, Radio buttons, and another Selection list.
- Change the tags to resize the text box and make it larger.
- Instead of the <HR> lines, add your own graphical line breaks.
- Add a background or other graphics to enhance your page.

Debriefing

You have created a Web form with text blocks, Radio buttons, Check boxes, a Selection list, and a text box. Form pages will be important as you create your Web pages to gather information from the Web, and have them processed on a server to give you information.

Here are my official HTML notes from this activity:

1. To create a text block, use the following tag:

    <TEXTAREA NAME="" TYPE="" COLS= ROWS= >. This tag begins the text box and sets up the TYPE as TEXT. The size of the box is determined with COLUMNS=? and ROWS=?. If you want the box bigger, you need to insert larger numbers for ?.

    </TEXTAREA> turns off the text area.

2. A Check box is created with the following tag:

    The <INPUT TYPE="CHECKBOX" VALUE=""> tag creates a small box to check. The difference between this and the Radio button is that Radio buttons are used for one choice, while check boxes are used for all that apply.

3. Selection lists are a great way to conserve space. They are created with these tags:

    The tag <SELECT NAME="Type of Food"> creates a Selection list.

    <OPTION SELECTED> inserts the item, which in this activity is Pizza, as the current choice in the window.

    The tag <OPTION> lists items to choose from, when the window is activated.

4. To create a Submit or Reset button, use the following tags:

    The tag <INPUT TYPE="SUBMIT" VALUE="Submit Information"> creates a button used to send the information to a server to be processed. Since your page is not connected to a Web server, and a file has not been created to process this information, this button will not currently work.

    If you would like more information on creating the file that processes this information, please visit the link on the Activity 20 page titled "C++ Programming."

    The tag <INPUT TYPE="RESET" VALUE="Reset Forms Page"> creates a button to reset the form. If information is entered incorrectly, or if another person using the same browser wants to enter their information, they can reset the form with this button.

Notes for Word Users:

If you are using Internet Assistant for Word, you can create all sorts of form tools, boxes and lists. There isn't enough room to teach you all of the ways Word has to help you. So, it is time to dust off the Help files and see how much the Internet Assistant for Word Help can assist you.

1. Click the Help menu and select **Internet Assistant for Microsoft Word Help** from the pull-down menu.

2. Click the Index tab.

3. Enter Forms in the help text window and click display.

4. Read the options.

5. The Help menus will direct you as you explore the features. If you click the Insert menu you will see the Form Field option.

6. See if you can locate various form creation tools as shown in Figure A20-2. This tool palette will allow you to create all sorts of buttons and form fields.

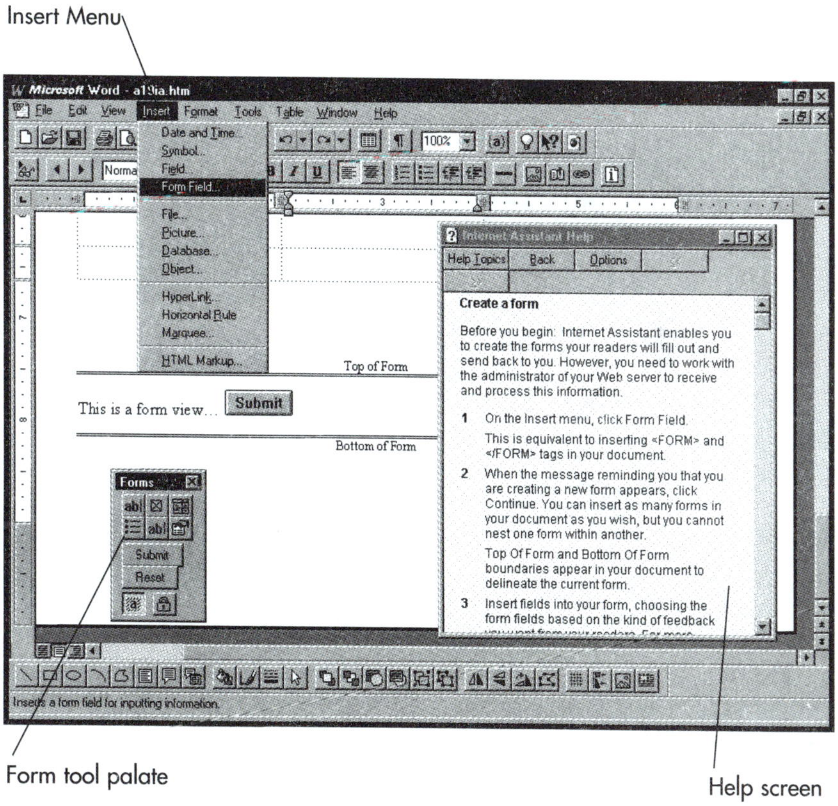

Figure A20-2
Use the Internet Assistant for Word Help Menus to Learn about Form Tools

Insert Menu

Form tool palate

Help screen

Cartoons of the Web

"As I have visited different Web pages, I have also noticed cartoon animations appearing everywhere. The Web is alive with movement! Upon further investigation, I have found these to be called animated GIFs."

"To create motion, several drawings are shown quickly, one right after another. The different drawings, if placed consecutively and correctly, can create the illusion of movement."

"Many animated GIFs are in a continuous loop. Once you have seen it, the Web page will reload it and start over. You are constantly going back to get the same file continually."

Table of Tags for Activity 21		
Image Search	<IMG SRC=" ">	Locate an animated GIF.

"I have collected some animated GIFs from the Web during my investigations; several are on my Web page, others can be found by selecting several hypertext links."

Objectives:

- Visit selected sites on the Web and view animated GIFs.
- Download several animated GIFs to use in a Web page.
- Create a Web page using animated GIFs.

Understanding Animated GIFs

Step 1: Load your Web browser and locate the *HTML Activities Web Page.* Select the <u>Activity 21</u> link.

Step 2: Can you see the small dog? He seems to be busy. Also, you should see a small picture of children playing on a swing.

2A: Take a few minutes and click on the links under the title **My Animated Collection.**

2B: As you go to each of the animated GIF screens, give them a chance to load and begin their movement.

Downloading Animated GIFs

Step 3: Animated GIFs can be downloaded the same way regular images are downloaded. If you need help, refer to Activity 9.

NOTE: As we talked about in Activity 15, you need to be careful about taking information from the Web. Just as books are copyrighted, text, graphics, and pictures on the Web can also be copyrighted. If you are interested in getting a graphic, make sure you read the page completely for any copyright information.

Activity 21 Animate Your Web Page

3A: Locate the small dog running across the screen. Point your mouse at the area the dog is running in and click your right mouse button in Windows or hold your mouse key down on a Macintosh.

3B: If you do not remember how to complete the downloading of an image, refer to Activity 9.

3C: Save the file in your **projects/graphics** directory or folder with the file name **dogrun.gif** .

3D: Choose **File, Open** from your browser's menu bar.

3E: Change to the directory **projects**, and then the sub-directory **graphics**. Choose the file you saved, **dogrun.gif**.

This file should load into your browser and the small dog should be running back and forth across your screen. If you are not getting the file to work correctly, repeat Steps 1-3 and download the graphic again.

Time for a Field Trip

Step 4: Now it is time to gather a few animated GIFs. I have selected several great sites to locate and view animated GIFs.

4A: From the Activity 21 link, locate the heading **Going on a Field Trip.**

4B: Use the listed links to surf the Web and look at, download, and save interesting images. This may take awhile, especially when you see the fun you can have watching animation on the Web. When you get back from your field trip, we'll use the animated GIFs you downloaded in a Web page.

4C: You will need to locate and download at least three noncopyrighted animated GIFs from the Web before you continue with Step 5.

Placing Animated GIFs in Your Page

Step 5: Now that you have returned, it's time to use your images in an actual page:

5A: Load your HTML or text editor and insert the starting HTML tags.

5B: Enter the title <TITLE> My Animated GIFS</TITLE>.

5C: Choose an appropriate background from your **graphics** sub-directory for this page and add the tag:

<BODY BACKGROUND="graphics/xxxxxxxx.???">

5D: In the body of your document, create a heading with the <H1> tag that reads: My Collection. It should also be centered.

<CENTER>
<H1>My Collection </H1>
</CENTER>

5E: Under the </CENTER> tag, insert your first animated GIF. Use the same tag you would use when loading a normal GIF:

<IMG SRC="graphics/name of file.GIF">

5F: Under the tag in Step 5E, insert two more tags to load two additional GIFs you found.

5G: Save the file in your **projects** directory as **animate.htm** or **animate.html**.

Step 6: Close your HTML Editor and load your Web browser.

6A: Open the file **animate.htm** or **animate.html.**

6B: Your animated page should load and your animated images should begin to move, dance, or whatever they were designed to do.

Step 7: Go back to your animated Web page and insert more of the images you gathered. Change the size of the image, the alignment, and insert text to tell the viewer about the GIF. Save your page again and view it in your Web browser.

Troubleshooting

If you are having trouble with your animated GIFs, try the following:

- Load a different GIF to try.
- Make sure your IMG SRC tag is pointed to the correct directory.
- Understand that GIF animation will act differently on slower or faster machines.

Extension: If you have time, try the following:

- Locate a shareware or freeware GIF animator program on the Net.
- Use a search engine to locate your own animated GIF Web pages.
- Post your animated GIFs on your own Web site for others to visit.

Debriefing

GIF animation is just one of the exciting parts of Web exploration. In the next activity, we will discover pages that use Shockwave and Java and Java Scripting to increase the functionality of the Web pages. As you view the different parts of the Web, take note of the many aspects that make up the Web — tags, images, frames, forms, animation, ShockWave, and Java. It's an exciting place to be!

Here are my official HTML notes from this activity:

1. Animated GIFs are the same as cartoon characters. Many still images create movement when sequenced and shown together.

2. You can create your own animated GIFs to display on your Web page. Programs to create these images can be found on the Web and downloaded to your computer.

3. Animated GIFs create motion in a Web page. By creating motion, you may create an interest for people to return.

We're Not in HTML Anymore, Toto!

The Internet traffic is getting busy. Like a growing city, new roads, new services, and new innovations are constantly being added. Java, JavaScripts, Shockwave, and VRML are recent, new additions to the Internet community.

Java gives the programmer the ability to send a small file, or applet, as they are called, to run on a personal computer. JavaScripts allow the same sort of programs to be created, only the scripts are written within the Web page. Shockwave allows multimedia presentations to be displayed. Each of these innovations adds interest to the Web environment. VRML is an acronym for Virtual Reality Modeling Language. This application allows three-dimensional objects to be created.

Table of Tags for Activity 22		
To Begin and End Java	<SCRIPT> </SCRIPT>	To begin and end a script, you must begin with the tag <SCRIPT Language="JavaScript">. Then, insert the script you would like to run.
To Run a Java Applet	<APPLET> </APPLET>	To begin a Java applet, you must use the <APPLET> tag.

O b j e c t i v e s :

- Visit sites that have Shockwave, Java, VRML, and JavaScript applications.
- Read the source code to Shockwave, Java, VRML, and JavaScript.
- Create a Web page to your favorite Shockwave, Java, VRML, and JavaScript pages.

Note: Before you begin this activity, verify your ability to view Java, JavaScript, and Shockwave applications in your Web browser.

 Step 1:

To view various Java, JavaScript, VRML, and Shockwave applications:

1A: Load your Web browser and locate the *HTML Activities Web Page.*

1B: Choose the Activity 22 link.

1C: Locate the Java Clock link and click it.

"This is the Java applet I have been working on. It is not quite ready yet, but I will let you have the first look at it. I wanted to have a digital clock on the Web, just like the clock on my desk. You can even see that it has the correct time — well, for my time zone anyway! If the clock works for you, you're ready to visit the Web and find more Java applets."

Step 2: Return to the <u>Activity 22</u> page. Under the <u>Java Clock</u> link, there is a listing of Java, Shockwave, VRML, and JavaScript sites on the Net. Take a few minutes and choose the links. They will take you to places that have Java applet games, graphics, and even programs.

Creating your Best of the Web Page

Step 3: After you have finished your evaluation of these pages, and possibly even located new ones using search engines, you are ready to create your Best of the Web page.

3A. Exit your Web browser and load your HTML Editor.

3B: Insert the basic starting HTML tags.

3C: Your title should be <TITLE>Best of the Web</TITLE>.

3D: Use an appropriate background from your **graphics** directory.

3E: Create a centered heading <H2> that reads My Best of the Web.

```
<CENTER>
<H2>My Best of the Web</H2>
</CENTER>
```

3F: Download and insert a <HR> line or a graphical bar before you begin your list of the Best of the Web.

Step 4: Create your best five Java, VRML, JavaScript, or Shockwave hypertext links.

4A: Create a heading <H3> under the <HR> that reads Java, JavaScript, VRML, and Shockwave on the Web.

```
<P>
<H3>Java, JavaScript, VRML, and ShockWave on the
Web</H3><BR>
```

4B: Create five hypertext links, each divided by a <BR>, of your best sites.

4C: After your last link, close your document with the </BODY> and </HTML> tags.

Step 5: Save your file as **java.htm** or **java.html** in your **projects** folder.

Step 6: Close your HTML Editor and load your Web browser.

6A: Choose **File, Open File** from the pull-down menu.

6B: Locate your **java.htm** or **java.html** file and retrieve it.

"I am so excited about the page you created. It is great to have experienced HTML authors creating Web pages. Look at the page you just completed. Is there anything new you could do to this page? You are an experienced Webtop publisher now with ideas just waiting to come out."

Troubleshooting

If your page does not work:
- Check for spelling errors in your URLs.
- Make sure the hypertext links are correct.
- Make sure your browser is able to read Java, JavaScript, VRML, and Shockwave applications.

Extension: Want to stretch yourself? Try these:

- Create a table with your favorite links in different cells.

- Download a Java applet and load it in your Web page.

- Visit the Visual J++ page from the <u>Activity 22</u> link for more information about creating your own Java applications.

- Go out on the Web and try to find new innovations that allow video and sound to be displayed on the Web.

Debriefing

Shockwave, VRML, JavaScript, and Java allow a new level of creativity on the Web. Feel free to use a search engine to find out more about these and other important new innovations on the Web. These kinds of tools will allow the Web to continue to grow and become more and more powerful.

ags, Tags, Always Tags

"This book has taken you a long way in a short time. Just like investigative work, it is sometimes a good idea to backtrack where you have been. When you go over information you have already learned, you may uncover things you never saw the first time."

"The only limitation for creating a Web page will be your imagination. Given the same problem, many people will create different solutions depending on their knowledge and experiences. As you approach this activity, all of you will develop and create different types of Web pages."

"Review Appendix A if you need to review the various tags you need to use."

O b j e c t i v e s :

- Review tags and Web page creation.
- Use the IPTCP process.

It is time for one more challenge. Create a Web site totally of your own creation and design. Go for it! Use the IPTCP process to guide your work.

- **Investigate your topic.**
- **Plan your Web pages.**
- **Take a look around for ideas.**
- **Create your Webtop publications.**
- **Publish on the Web.**

Remember: This is your work and should be a reflection of you.

Debriefing

This activity has combined all of the tags and information you have learned and helped you create a great Web site. Congratulations!

Here are my official HTML notes for your successful mastery of *Webtop Publishing on the Superhighway*:

1. Great Job!
2. Great Job!!
3. Great Job!!!

 Activity 23 So, How Was That?

Appendix A

Summary of Tag Tables

Chapter 1: Activity 1: Starting Tags

Table of Tags for Activity 1		
HTML Tags	\<HTML>\</HTML>	Announces to the World Wide Web that this is an HTML document.
Header Tags	\<HEAD>\</HEAD>	Lets you enter special information about your Web page.
Title Tags	\<TITLE> \</TITLE>	Places a short title or description in a browser's title bar.
Body Tags	\<BODY>\</BODY>	Encloses the part of your Web page document that will actually be displayed by a Web browser. Anything not placed between the \<BODY> tags will not be displayed properly.

Chapter 2: Activities 2 and 3: Formatting Tags

Table of Tags for Chapter 2 and Activities 2 and 3		
Headings	<H1></H1> <H2></H2> <H3></H3> <H4></H4> <H5></H5> <H6></H6>	Heading tags make text appear larger or smaller depending on the number in the tag. <H1> allows the largest letters (or heading), while <H2> displays letters that are slightly smaller. The <H6> tag displays the smallest letters (or heading).
Paragraph Break (double-space)	<P>	This tag separates paragraphs by adding a line or a space. A closing tag </P> is optional.
Simple or Line Break (single space)	 	The tag creates a line break without adding an extra space between paragraphs.
Unordered List	<UL> <LI> <LI> <LI> </UL>	This sequence of tags creates bulleted lists, for example: • Something • Something • Something The UL is short for Unordered List. The LI tag means List.
Ordered List	<OL> <LI> <LI> <LI> </OL>	This sequence of tags creates numbered lists, for example: 1. Something 2. Something 3. Something The OL is short for Ordered List. The LI tag means List.
Center	<CENTER> </CENTER>	The <CENTER> tag centers the text in the browser window.

Chapter 3: Activity 5: Hyptertext Link Reference Tags

Table of Tags for Activity 5		
Anchor	<A></A>	The anchor tag. Used to create hypertext references.
Hypertext Reference	HREF=""	Hypertext REFerence. Used to indicate which URL, or Uniform Resource Locator, is being searched.

Chapter 3: Activity 7: Lines and Emphasis Tags

Table of Tags for Activity 7		
Horizontal Rule	<HR>	Create horizontal lines
Bold	<B>	Bold text
Italics	<I>	Italicize text
Emphasis	<EM>	Emphasize text (often italics)
Strong Emphasis	<STRONG>	Strongly emphasize text (often bold)

Chapter 3: Activity 8: Background Colors

Table of Tags for Activity 8		
Red	=Red or =ff0000	Color value for red
Green	=Green or =00ff00	Color value for green
Blue	=Blue or =0000ff	Color value for blue
White	=White or =ffffff	Color value for white
Black	=Black or =000000	Color value for black
Background Color	bgcolor	The Background Color attribute
Link Color	link	The Hypertext & Hyperlink Color attribute
Visited Link Color	vlink	The Visited Hypertext & Hyperlink attribute
Text Color	text	The Text Color attribute

Chapter 3: Activity 9: Image Tags

Table of Tags for Activity 9		
Image Search	<IMG SRC="">	Searches an image on your computer or on the Web.
Align Attribute	ALIGN=	Aligns pictures with the text.
Height Attribute	HEIGHT=	Determines the height of a graphic.
Width Attribute	WIDTH=	Determines the width of a graphic.

Chapter 6: Activity 15: Image Tags

Table of Tags for Activity 15		
Background Tags	<BODY BACKGROUND=" ">	Create a background for your HTML document.
Image Search Tags	<IMG SRC =" ">	Place a desired graphic into your HTML document.

Chapter 6: Activity 16:
Internal links or Internal Reference Anchors

Table of Tags for Activity 16		
Internal Links	<A HREF="#XXX"></A>	Internally links different parts of your HTML document. (Replace the XXX with a key word.)
Internal Anchors	<A NAME="XXX"></A>	Internal anchors create jumps in your HTML document. (Replace the XXX with a key word.)
Font Size	<FONT SIZE=+#></FONT>	Font Size lets you control the size of letters and text.

Chapter 6: Activity 17: Frame Tags

Table of Tags for Activity 17		
Frame Rows	<FRAMESET ROWS...>	Divides the browser window into horizontal frames.
Frame Columns	<FRAMESET COLS...>	Divides the browser window into vertical frames.
Turn Off Frame	</FRAMESET>	Used to turn off the Frame Settings.
Text Area	<BLOCKQUOTE>	Used to designate a block of text as a quote.
Loading URLs	TARGET="_top"	Used when you don't want to use frames to display the page.

Chapter 6: Activity 18: Table Tags

		Table of Tags for Activity 18
Beginning and Ending Table Tags	<TABLE> </TABLE>	These tags begin and end the table.
Table Title	<CAPTION> </CAPTION>	Similar to the <TITLE> tag, only creates a "title" for the table.
Create Rows	<TR></TR>	Table Row <TR> tags are used to create rows in the table.
Divide Rows into Columns	<TH></TH>	Table Headings <TH> divide rows into columns and describe each column of the table.
Table Data	<TD></TD>	Actual data of each cell of the table.

Chapter 6: Activity 19: Form Tags 1

		Table of Tags for Activity 19
Beginning and Ending Form Tags	<FORM METHOD></FORM>	These tags are used to begin and end the Forms section of your HTML document. Other tags for Radio buttons, Check boxes, and Lists can be inserted between these tags.
Type of Input Requested	<INPUT TYPE>	Defines the type of input allowed for the tag you are using.
Text Field	<INPUT TYPE="TEXT"	Defines the type of input or text information to be inserted.
Identifies the Field	NAME=" "	Displays prompt words on the browser screen.
Defines Size of Input Cell	SIZE=" "	Defines the size of the input area for text to be entered.
Radio Buttons	<INPUT TYPE="RADIO"	Displays a list of choices, with a selection button for each. Only one choice can be made.

Chapter 6: Activity 20: Form Tags 2

Table of Tags for Activity 20		
Check box Field in Forms	<INPUT TYPE= "CHECKBOX"	Type of input used in the Web page. This will create a Check box.
Selection List	<SELECT NAME=" "	Begins a Selection list of possible choices.
Selection Choice	<OPTION>	Gives a choice for the Selection list.
Written Text Field	<TEXTAREA NAME	Creates a text area. TYPE, COLS, ROWS contained in the tag are explained in the activity.
Submit Information	<INPUT TYPE= "SUBMIT"	Creates a button to submit information to the destination designated in ACTION.
Reset Information	<INPUT TYPE= "RESET"	Resets the forms page back to default.

Chapter 6: Activity 21:
Image Search tag for Animated .gif Files

Table of Tags for Activity 21		
Image Search	<IMG SRC=" ">	Locate an animated GIF.

Chapter 6: Activity 22: Applet and Script Tags

Table of Tags for Activity 22		
To Begin and End Java	<SCRIPT> </SCRIPT>	To begin and end a script, you must begin with the tag <SCRIPT Language="JavaScript">. Then, insert the script you would like to run.
To Run a Java Applet	<APPLET> </APPLET>	To begin a Java applet, you must use the <APPLET> tag.

Appendix B

Getting Your Pages Published or "Posted" on the World Wide Web

Most of your Webtop publishing creations have been created on your hard drive or on a floppy disk. This means you can view them, but others can't see your Web creations around the world on the Net. To view your Web pages on the WWW you will need to "post" your Webtop creations.

Before your Webtop creations can be viewed on the WWW, they need to be placed on a special Web server that is directly connected to the Internet. A Web server has special Web server software. This special server software allows visitors to access and view Web pages. This software makes use of a communications language called Hypertext Transfer Protocol, or HTTP.

There are several terms that are used by Webmasters to describe the process of putting pages on a Web server:

• Posting
• Uploading
• F-T-P-ing
• And the often used, "Putting it up there"

Webmasters oversee this process of posting and organizing files to Web servers. There are several ways to post pages and each Webmaster has their own special set of rules that bring order and organization to their Web server.

One of the key rules is to have your files organized. Normally, your graphics are kept in a separate folder or directory from your .htm or .html files. You learned how to organize your pages and graphics in Sector 3, Activity 15 when you set up your **projects** and **graphics** folders or directories. Check with your Webmaster on the specific instructions that govern your site.

Here are some of the most common ways to post:

• Some Webmasters have an on-line automatic web page creation form that users fill out. After the information is entered, a Web page is generated automatically using all the information on the form. This is a simple way to create Web pages, but you are not really Webtop publishing. You are simply filling in a standard form. Not much creativity is involved.

- Other Webmasters do all of the work for you. You can e-mail your HTML source code document (you know, the page with all the tags in it) as an attachment and your Webmaster can clean it up and put it on the Web for you.
- Your Webmaster can give you access directly to the Web server by means of an Internet tool called FTP. FTP is short for File Transfer Protocol. FTP lets you move files directly onto a Web server. Normally, your Webmaster gives you a space, called a directory or folder, on the Web server. When you place a Web page into that space, it is instantly viewable on the Web. FTP software is easy to use. FTP is a little like the Copy File command on your local computer. However, instead of making a copy of your file and moving it to a floppy disk or a hard drive, you are sending the file over the Internet to a folder or directory on a Web server computer. Your Webmaster can usually supply you with the instructions and the FTP software you need to reach the Web server.

When you use the FTP tool, you must recreate the folders or directories you have used in your Web pages. For example, in Activity 15 you created a **projects** and a **graphics** folder. You must upload all of your Web pages into directories of the same name on the Web server.

How URLs are Organized

There is one more thing your Webmaster must do for you. You must also obtain a URL or U̲niform R̲esource L̲ocator. You know what a URL is — that funny-looking Web address.

Your URL will look similar to the one shown below. Let's investigate the address for a second.

A - HTTP
B - Computer Name
C - Root Directory
D - Subdirectory
E - Filename

http://www.thomson.com/swpco/internet/markweb.html

A. The prefix http:// indicates that, to access this document, you need to use the Web's Hypertext Transfer Protocol built into your Web browser.

B. The next part of the address, www.thomson.com, is the specific name of the computer, or Web server where the Web page resides. The string www.thomson.com is also an example of a domain name.

C. The next part of the address, /swpco/, is a root or master folder or directory that you must open to find the page. In this case, swpco is an abbreviation or acronym of the publisher, South-Western Publishing Company.

D.	Since there are usually many, many Web pages on a single Web server, the different pages are organized in sub-folders called subdirectories separated by a slash (/). This subdirectory is appropriately called the /internet/.

E.	Finally, you get to the Web page document, also appropriately called markweb.html.

Getting your own URL can be as easy as asking your Webmaster, "What's my URL?" Just make sure you write it down!

After you have uploaded your files and graphics into folders or directories on the Web server, you are ready to hop out to the Web and view how things look. You will find errors and mistakes. Use your trouble-shooting skills to fix your pages and correct all the links.

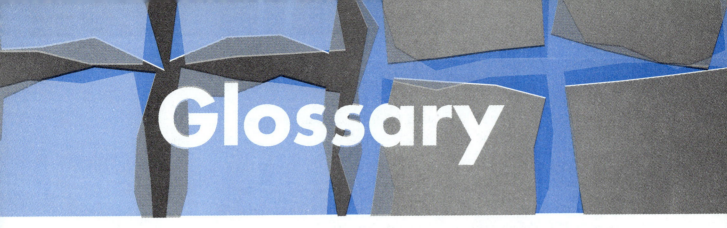

Glossary

.gif: Graphics Interchange Format. One of the most widely used graphics formats on the World Wide Web. Created by CompuServe.

.htm: A file extension used by DOS and Windows computers to identify HTML documents to Web browsers.

.html: A file extension used by Windows 95 or higher, Macintosh, and UNIX computers to identify HTML documents to Web browsers.

.jpeg: Joint Photographic Expert Group. The Joint Photographic Expert Group was an international committee that defined this standard graphics file format. This graphics format is widely used on the Web.

.jpg: See .jpeg.

.txt: A file extension that indicates the file is a text document.

Angle brackets: Angle brackets identify HTML commands to Web browsers. Angle brackets look like this: < >

Applets: Applets are executable programs written for the World Wide Web using the Java programming language.

ASCII: American Standard Code for Information Interchange. Includes standard characters that all computers can read and understand. They include the letters, numbers, and symbols found on the keyboard, and other characters.

Attributes: Attributes are commands to a Web browser that state what kind of operation is required. For example, the attribute BGCOLOR= tells the browser to display a background color. (*See also* Values.)

Bookmarks: Bookmarks provide Netscape users with a way to list their favorite Web pages so they can return to them easily. Internet Explorer users call this feature "Favorites."

Brackets: See Angle brackets.

Browse: On the Web, browse is another word for surf or search.

Browser: A browser or Web browser is a software tool that searches and displays HTML and other documents and graphics from the Internet and World Wide Web. The most popular browsers are Netscape and Internet Explorer.

Bundled: Bundled means grouped together. If software is bundled with a book, it means the software comes with the book.

CGI: Common Gateway Interface. CGI allows users to interact with Web pages. For example, with CGI you can create forms, have Web visitors enter data into the form, and have that data processed. CGI is a recognized standard for interfacing applications, like database programs, with Web servers and Web pages.

Close tags: Close tags end HTML commands. Close tags are easy to spot because of the identifying forward slash as in </CENTER>.

Compelling Web site: A compelling Web site is one that visitors want to visit again and again.

Cyberspace: A term used to describe the Internet and the World Wide Web.

Directory: *See also* subdirectory and folder. A directory is a term used to describe a logical place to save electronic files on computer hard drives, CDs, or diskettes. On the Web, directories are separated by slashes. For example, /swpco in the following example is a directory: http://www.thomson.com/swpco/internet/markweb.html

DOS: Disk Operating System.

Extensions: Extensions are identifiers for file names. For example, the extension .htm or .html identifies HTML documents. The file extension .txt often identifies text documents. The extension .doc identifies Word documents, and the extension .wpd identifies WordPerfect documents.

FAQ: Internet talk for Frequently Asked Questions.

Favorites: Favorites is the term the Internet Explorer uses for bookmarks or hotlists. (See Bookmarks.)

File extensions: See Extensions.

Flame: A written rebuke over the Internet.

Folder: A term often used for a directory or subdirectory. A logical place to save files, graphics, and data.

Formatting tags: Formatting tags add interest to Web pages. They include commands that can be compared to the word processing commands like bold <B>, italic <I>, bigger <H1> or smaller <H6> letters, Center <CENTER>, left <LEFT>, and right <RIGHT> justify.

Freeware: Software that anyone can use freely. Freeware can be downloaded from the Internet.

FTP: File Transfer Protocol. FTP is used to transfer files and data from one computer to another on the Internet.

Graphics: Graphics are pictures in an electronic format. The most popular graphics formats on the Web are .gif and .jpeg. (*See also* .gif and .jpeg.)

GUI: Graphical User Interface. GUI simply means pictures or icons are substituted for words on a computer interface. For example, the command CUT is often replaced by a picture of a pair of scissors.

HEX: See Hexadecimal.

Hexadecimal: A numbering system based on 16 rather than 10. Hexadecimal uses the letters A, B, C, D, E, and F along with numbers 0 to 9 to create new number combinations.

Home page: A Home page is usually the starting page of a Web site. Many people call all Web pages Home pages. While not technically correct, every qualified Web surfer understands that both terms are often used interchangeably. (See Web page.)

HTML Editor: A specialized text editor that allows users to enter HTML tags quickly and easily.

HTML: See Hypertext Markup Language.

Hyperlinks: Hyperlinks include both words and pictures that are referenced to other Web pages or pieces of Internet information. Hyperlinks send you to new and related information.

Hypertext links: Hypertext links are words that "link" or send you out to cyberspace for other related Web pages of information. Hypertext links are usually underlined or appear in a different color.

Hypertext Markup Language: The language of the World Wide Web, HTML uses tags or commands in angle brackets (< >) to instruct Web browsers how to display documents and graphics on the Web.

Internet: A worldwide network of networks connecting millions of servers and computer users together.

Internet Assistant for Word: Created by Microsoft, Internet Assistant is the popular word processing program's HTML Editor. Easy to use. Internet Assistant is now bundled with Word or can be downloaded from Microsoft.

Internet Explorer: Microsoft's popular Web browser.

Internet Publisher: Corel WordPerfect's HTML Editor.

ISP: See Internet Service Provider.

Internet Service Provider: An Internet Service Provider (ISP) is a company or organization that provides access to the Internet and World Wide Web. The largest ISP today is America Online, or AOL. There are many others, both large and small, including Microsoft Network (MSN), Prodigy, and CompuServe.

Java: A programming language adapted to the needs of the Internet and World Wide Web. Java programs for the Web are called applets.

JavaScript: Not to be confused with the Java programming language, JavaScript takes advantage of the capabilities of the browser to read tags and commands. JavaScript allows Java-like programs to be written directly into an HTML document.

Links: See Hypertext links and Hyperlinks.

Lowercase: Lowercase letters are small letters, not CAPITAL LETTERS.

Net: Short for Internet. See Internet.

Netscape: A popular Web browser.

Notepad: Text editor found on Windows computers. Notepad saves files in a simple text format with a .txt extension.

Open tags: Tags that start an option or an HTML command.

PageMill: The first WYSIWYG HTML Editor created by Adobe.

Post: See Posting.

Posting: The act of uploading or transferring HTML Web pages to a Web server to be displayed on the World Wide Web. Pages are normally uploaded using FTP or File Transfer Protocol. FTP is to the Internet what the copy feature is on your computer operating system software.

Public Domain: When pictures and stories are in the public domain, it means that anyone can use them for the purposes for which they were intended. For example, "The Star Spangled Banner" is public. You can sing or record it without paying someone for the privilege of using it. Graphics that are in the public domain can be copied and used on web pages.

Refresh: Nearly every browser has a Refresh or Reload feature that allows you to try to load a Web page that may have appeared with errors in it. Refresh is the term use with the Internet Explorer browser.

Reload: Nearly every browser has a Reload feature that allows you to reload or refresh a Web page. If a page comes in too slow or appears with errors in it, Reload or Refresh will try the page again, often fixing the previously viewed problems. Reload is the term used with the Netscape browser.

RESPECT: Short for Responsible, Everybody, Simplicity, Purpose, Ethical Use, Correctness, and Totally Cool — a series of tests Webmasters can use to guide their development of Web sites.

Search engine: Software on the Web that allows a user to search for key words or topics. Search engines search Web pages for information related to the words entered into the search request.

Server: A special computer that shares files with other computers over a network. Servers serve files or documents and graphics to client computers. Client computers request files or documents and graphics from servers.

Shareware: Software that users can download and try free of charge for a trial period of time. However, if they decide they like the software and want to keep it, they must pay a fee to continue using it.

Shockwave: Shockwave is software that plays and distributes multimedia programs created with Macromedia Director over the Web. Both Shockwave and Macromedia Director are available through Macromedia at www.macromedia.com.

SimpleText: Text editor found on Macintosh computers. SimpleText saves files in a simple text format.

Slash: A slash is a line that separates file and directory names. This is a slash (/). There are actually two kinds of slashes, a forward slash (/) and a backward slash (\). The Web uses forward slashes (/), for example: http://www.thomson.com/swpco/internet/markweb.html

Starting tags: Starting tags appear in every HTML document and include the following tags in the following order:
<HTML><HEAD><TITLE></TITLE></HEAD><BODY></BODY></HTML>

Subdirectory: (*See also* Directory and Folder.) A subdirectory is a term used to describe a directory or folder inside another directory or folder. Subdirectories are logical places to save electronic files on computer hard drives, CDs, or diskettes. On the Web, subdirectories are separated by slashes. In the example below, /internet is a subdirectory in the /swpco directory:
http://www.thomson.com/swpco/internet/markweb.html

Tags: Tags are used in HTML to signal commands and instructions to Web browsers. Tags mark a document in ways that instruct the browser to display the document in specific ways. Tags appear in angle brackets like this, <TAG>.

Text editor: A text editor like Notepad or SimpleText allows the user to type words and text characters and save them in a text file format.

Text export: Saving a file as a text file requires the host software to perform a translation of the file into a text format often called a text export.

Text file: A file saved in a text format, usually with extensions like .txt, .htm, or .html.

Toolbars: Toolbars are made up of buttons that usually appear at the top of most software programs. Normally a series of icons or pictures, toolbar buttons give you one click access to commonly used software commands. For example, nearly every software browser has a stop button on its toolbar.

Truncated file names: File names, particularly in DOS, are often shortened. These "truncated" file names may change a file name like GETTYSBERGADDRESS.TEXT to GETTYSBE.TXT.

Uniform Resource Locator: A Uniform Resource Locator, or URL, is an address used to find documents on the World Wide Web. A URL can be a series of words or numbers separated by periods and slashes. For example: http://www.thomson.com/swpco/internet/markweb.html or http://159.91.6.2/MyStuff/file.html

UNIX: Important mainframe computer operating system software/ platform. UNIX computers are widely used on the Web because they are fast and generally reliable. UNIX was created by the Bell Labs and many versions of it are free.

Uppercase: Uppercase letters are CAPITAL LETTERS.

URL: See Uniform Resource Locator.

Values: Values define attributes. For example, for the attribute BGCOLOR=, many color values can be defined. Words like WHITE, or RED, or BLUE can be values. Values can also be numbers, like FFFFFF for White, FF0000 for Red, and 0000FF for Blue.

Web browser: See Browser.

Web server: A special computer that contains Web pages that Web users can access and view. (See also Server.)

Web site: A series of interrelated Web pages on a particular topic constitutes a Web site. Companies like Microsoft have extensive Web sites dedicated to their company products and services. Schools can also have Web sites or collections of Web pages created by their students.

Web page: A Web page is a page of information created in HTML and displayed on the World Wide Web. Also called Home page or Web document.

Web document: See Web page.

Webmaster: A Webmaster is the guardian of a Web server. These people manage Web pages, Web sites, and Internet services.

Word: A very popular word processing program written and owned by Microsoft. Word has a built-in or "bundled" HTML Editor called the Internet Assistant.

WordPerfect: A very popular word processing program owned by Corel that has a built-in or "bundled" HTML Editor called the Internet Publisher.

World Wide Web: A series of computers that use and understand HTTP, or Hypertext Transfer Protocol. These computers transmit HTML documents to Web users around the world.

Wraparound: Text editors and word processors with a wraparound feature will automatically shift the text down when the end of the line is reached. Some text editors do not have a wraparound feature, so the user must press Enter or Return at the end of each line of text.

WWW: See World Wide Web.

WYSIWYG: What You See Is What You Get. WYSIWYG approximates on the computer screen what will result in real life. For example, when typing a letter, a WYSIWYG word processing program will display on the monitor what will be printed on a printer.

Index

Java Clock link, 155
JavaScript, 77, 155, 171
Joint Photographic Expert
    Group (.jpg, .jpeg), 42, 116,
    168

L

Lines and Emphasis tags, 161
Links. *See also hypertext links*
    appear as, 53
    background and links
        command, 95
    changing colors, 95
    color attributes, 61-62
    creating internal, 122, 126,
        129
    faster links, 93
    locating, 43-46
    making, 53-56
    to anchors, 122-129
    visited link (vlink), 62
Lists, 26-28
    hypertext, 50
    making changes to, 27
    ordered, 26, 27
    selection list, 148
    unordered, 26, 27
Lowercase, 171

M

Macintosh
    file extensions, 13
    Save As, 12, 17, 30
Microsoft Corporation, 13
    browsers, 108
    creating standards, 109
Mosaic,103, 108

N

Net. *See Internet*
Netscape, 171
    bookmarks menu, 46
    file menu, 18-19
    icon, 44
    Open Window, 19
    Reload, 21
    Save Picture As, 65
    toolbar buttons, 45
    view, 39
    View Source command, 40

Notepad, vi, 10,171
    icon, 11
    starting, 15
    .txt files, 29
Notes, viii

O

Open tags, 171
Ordered list tags, 26, 28

P

PageMill, 171
Paragraph tags, 25, 28
Personal Information on the
    Web, 16
Picture dialog box, 97-98
Plagiarism, 117
Posting on the Web, 36, 171,
    110, 165
Programming languages, 76
Public Domain, 67, 171

R

Radio buttons, 141, 145
Refresh, 21, 171
Reload, 21, 171
Reset button, 149-150
RESPECT tests, 111-114
    defined, 171

S

Save As
    dialog box, 118
    Macintosh, 12, 17
    Windows, 12, 17
Scanned pictures, 64
Script tags, 164
Search engine, 80, 171
    start search button, 142
Selection list, 150
Server, 6,171
Shareware, 74, 172
Shockwave, 76, 155, 172
SimpleText, vi, 11, 15, 172
Slash, 31, 41, 172
Standard and formatting tool-
    bars for Word, 88
Starting tags, 159, 172
Strong emphasis tag, 57
Subdirectory, 172. *See also*
    Directory and Folder

Submit button, 149-150
Summary of tag tables,
    159-164

T

Tables
    changing borders, 139
    rows and columns, 136
    setting up, 136
    using HTML editor, 138
    tags, 163
    troubleshooting, 139
Tags
    anchor ,48
    attributes, 40
    blockquote, 135
    body, x, 14
    bold , 57, 59
    break, 25-26, 28
    case, 9, 32
    center, 24, 28
    defined, 172
    emphasis, 57, 59
    font size, 122
    form method, 141
    formatting, 24, 160
    frame columns, 132
    frame rows. 132
    H1 to H6, 24-25
    header, x, 14
    headings, 28
    hidden, 7
    horizontal rule, 57
    HTML, x, 14
    input type, 141
    internal anchors, 122
    internal links, 122
    italics, 57, 59
    list, 26
    ordered list, 26, 28
    paragraph, 25-26, 28
    radio buttons, 141
    size of input cell, 141
    starting, 8-9, 15
    strong emphasis, 57, 59
    text area, 132
    text field, 141
    title, x, 14
    turn frame, 132
    unordered list, 26, 28
    values, 40